THE CLASS OF '45

THE CLASS OF '45

authorHOUSE®

AuthorHouse™
1663 Liberty Drive
Bloomington, IN 47403
www.authorhouse.com
Phone: 1 (800) 839-8640

Published by AuthorHouse 09/01/2015

ISBN: 978-1-5049-3293-6 (sc)
ISBN: 978-1-5049-3294-3 (e)

Roosevelt campus was surrounded by barbed wire for the duration of the war

Roosevelt High School Class of '45

A compilation of 14 memoirs of members of this special class that spent all of its high school years during World War II in Hawaii's only English Standard high school.

Compiled by:
Barbara Dorsam Del Piano, Class of '45
2015

TABLE OF CONTENTS

Acknowledgements xi
Introduction xiii
Prologue xv

Theodora "Teddy" Lee Chang 1
James Macklin Hill, Jr. 6
Yvonne Neely Armitage Hodgins 11
Donald Ching 19
Janice Amante Hobson Monro 27
Charles Amor 33
Lorraine "Brownie" Brown Williams 39
School Days..46
Dexter Dickson 52
Elizabeth Hironaka Rathburn 57
James Benjamin Seelig 63
Georgia Schultz Rush..68
Quai Lum Young D.D.S., M.S.P.H. 75
Ellen Kawamoto Shikuma 80
William "Tex" Hays 86

Epilogue 91
Glossary Of Hawaiian Words 93

ACKNOWLEDGEMENTS

Many thanks to the fourteen classmates who participated in this project and to Sally Hill for the countless hours she spent editing and proof reading. To Betty Lemke Dower who offered her company's copy machine for the many copies required and to Georgia Rush for her invaluable financial assistance. And a big mahalo to my grandson, Brian Madariaga who helped prepare the manuscript for the publisher.

Mahalo nui loa,

Barbara Dorsam Del Piano

INTRODUCTION

Assembling these memoirs has truly been a labor of love. As a member of the Roosevelt High School Class of '45, I had no idea at the time what diverse backgrounds my classmates came from. It was not until Donald Ching unexpectedly passed away in 2009, and copies of his memoirs were distributed at his funeral service, that I realized that our class held a great deal of history, not only of the years of World War II, but also of early immigrants to Hawai'i.

These memoirs relate the lives of a random group of classmates from ancestry, through early childhood and adolescence, with heavy emphasis on December 7th, 1941. They describe their high school years and end with graduation in 1945. What makes this class unique is that Roosevelt was the only English Standard high school in Hawai'i; the class also spent all its years during World War II.

PROLOGUE

After a closure of nearly four months, due to the bombing of Pearl Harbor and America's entering World War II, students in the freshman class at Roosevelt High assembled for the first time at their new school. Entering through an opening in the barbed wire that surrounded the campus, carrying gasmasks over their shoulders, and initially feeling a bit apprehensive, most found the adjustment surprisingly easy. Many had come from Stevenson Intermediate, an English Standard school; some from as far away as Waialua. Others had transferred from Maryknoll, a Catholic coed school, and 'Iolani, a boys' school operated by the Episcopal Church.

The English Standard system originated in 1924 when *haole* parents complained that their children were not receiving a proper education because of the presence of so many non-English speaking children in their classes. In answer to their wishes, the Department of Education established Lincoln Elementary School. Centrally located on Beretania Street, it was the first public school in Hawai'i where non-*haole* students were required to pass both an oral and written English Language exam in order to be accepted. Lincoln was followed by other English Standard elementary schools, including Thomas Jefferson in Waikīkī, Ali'iolani in Kaimukī, and August Ahrens in Waipahu. There were also schools on the neighbor islands, primarily catering to the children of plantation management.

In 1930, the demand for an English Standard high school resulted in the construction of the imposing red-tiled Spanish-style building erected on the slopes of Punchbowl. Completed in 1932, it first opened as a junior high school; later, the ninth grade was eliminated when Robert Louis Stevenson was established, offering classes to seventh, eighth, and ninth graders. Roosevelt's first graduating class was in 1935.

In retrospect, English Standard schools were discriminatory; they were eliminated in 1960. However, for students at Roosevelt during that time, there were advantages. One in particular was that it brought together students from all parts of the island, and other islands as well, and gave them an opportunity to mix academically and socially with different ethnic groups and to become acquainted with the many cultures they represented.

Another plus was that parents, who could not afford to send their children to Punahou or other private schools, were assured that their children received a high quality education. Curriculum, teaching staff, physical facilities and extracurricular activities were all at top level. Although a part of its campus was taken over by the U. S. Navy during the war, Roosevelt was not subjected to nearly as many disruptions as most other schools.

The entire Punahou campus, consisting of more than seventy-six acres, was taken over by the U. S. Army Corps of Engineers. (There is a story that has circulated ever since, that in the confusion following the Pearl Harbor attack, Punahou was mistakenly confiscated; the original intent was to take over McKinley.) Farrington, another public high school, St. Louis College, a private Catholic boys' school, and the Kamehameha Schools for Boys and Girls were turned into hospitals for wounded troops. Those schools held classes elsewhere. Although the Roosevelt campus was surrounded by barbed wire and the U.S. Navy had possession of the gymnasium and athletic field, school activities were carried on, although under war-time restrictions.

Each Monday, students were required to perform manual labor in the pineapple fields of Wahiawā; if, for medical or other reasons, they were unable to withstand the hardships involved, they worked either at the Dole pineapple cannery or in the school office. Students had to carry gas masks with them at all times, and air raid drills were a common occurrence.

The teaching staff consisted of mostly mainland-born middle-aged *haole* spinsters who dressed with decorum. The principal, Robert Spencer, was a male, as were a few teachers including some who were in the armed forces. The school counselor, Nina Wise, was part-Hawaiian and greatly admired for her fair but firm attitude, and genuine concern for the students.

Surprisingly, the number of Chinese students equaled that of the Caucasians, each comprising approximately 26 % of the student body. They were followed by Japanese at 14 %, part-Hawaiian at 12 %, Portuguese at 8 % and Koreans at 6 %. There were three Filipinos in the class and the remainder of the students were of mixed nationalities. There was one pure Hawaiian, one of Spanish ancestry, and a sailor who was stationed on the campus and allowed to attend classes.

There is no evidence of any racial discrimination existing at Roosevelt. Although specific ethnic groups tended to congregate with each other during recess at a particular place on the campus, and socialize with each other after school, they had no trouble in class or participating in extra-curricular activities where students of all ethnicities were involved. Class officers and members of the various academic clubs, as well as sports teams, including football, basketball, track, and swimming, were comprised of students of every race.

It might even be noted that ethnic foods, such as Japanese *saimin* and *tempura,* Chinese *dim sum* and crack seed, Hawaiian *pipi kaula* and *poi*, Portuguese *malasadas* and sweet bread, and Korean *kim chee* were popular among all the students, not to mention *haole* hot dogs and hamburgers.

Today, Roosevelt High School, like all public schools in the Islands, is restricted to students living in a designated district near that school. Gone are the days when students from Kailua, Waialua, Waipahu, Kalihi, or Kaua'i were given the opportunity to acquaint themselves with different cultures and customs, and to gain a life-long appreciation of the diversity that makes up our special "Island Style." Those who attended the school in those days, of whatever ethnicity, are grateful for the opportunity to have been a part of the system and for the superior education they received.

Theodora "Teddy" Lee Chang

I was born in Honolulu to very humble Chinese parents who had no more than a fifth grade education. My dad was an orphan who came to Hawai'i from Shanghai as a "paper" son. This means he entered the country illegally with papers of a dead boy. He had been adopted by distant relatives and came under the guise of their deceased son. My mother was born in Punalu'u, O'ahu, where her father worked as a rice farmer.

There were four children in our family; my older brother, Kenneth, was two years older than I. I was the second to arrive, followed in eleven and a half months by brother, Charlie. He too was only eleven and a half months old when the last, our sister, Jenny, was born. I mention all this because our mother had all four of us by age twenty-six, and three of us were in diapers at the same time.

When Jenny's birthday arrived on June eleventh, she was the same age as Charlie for two weeks. Then Charlie, who celebrated his birthday on June twenty-sixth, was my age for two weeks. At this point, Jenny and I were a year apart and we had a brother in between us who was not a twin.

When I was six years old, Father decided that working at the Del Monte Cannery was not his life's goal. He set his mind on being his own boss and bought Lanikai Market in Kailua on the windward side of O'ahu. Soon after, our parents moved to Kailua to run the market. The small general store was located on a fairly large piece of property, and in addition to the market, there was a house and small warehouse. Dad bought a truck so that he could pick up supplies each week.

Our parents wanted us to attend Chinese language school, which was held daily from 3:00 pm to 5:00 pm, after English school. We three older children stayed with Aunty and Uncle Luke, mother's sister and her husband, who were willing to board us at their home in Kalihi during school days. Jenny, the youngest, stayed with our parents and was raised by them in Kailua.

Aunty, mother's older sister, was a stay-at-home mom. She had five youngsters in her home and didn't encourage us to invite friends over, nor did she allow us to go to other homes. Uncle's parents also lived in the small house, but we all managed to get along nicely. Aunty treated me as a Chinese girl in the culture of the times. I had to do housework, and later, when two more cousins were born, I babysat them while I longed to join the four boys riding bikes, roller skating, climbing trees, and playing ball. I couldn't participate in any of these activities, and many times I wished I were a boy.

At the age of six, I started first grade at Fern School. I remember being very lonesome during recess as I didn't make friends easily. It was a traumatic experience; I had lived a sheltered life and didn't know how to cope in this new environment. The teacher had to call on my brother, Ken, to keep me company and comfort me during recess. I must have been a gigantic headache to him. However, once I became accustomed to the school routine, I thoroughly embraced it; I loved reading and all the other academic activities.

After finishing third grade at Fern School, I transferred to Kapālama School, an English Standard School which was a long walk from our home near Fort Shafter. To qualify for entry, you had to pass an English speaking test; no "pidgin English" was allowed. My three years at Kapālama were great fun. I remember being asked to monitor the class whenever there was a teacher's meeting when school was in session. Today I marvel at how well-behaved the entire class was. This couldn't happen today!

Another great honor was being chosen to be a Junior Police Officer. Our job was to hold STOP signs in front of the school to halt the cars so students could cross the street safely.

Chinese school wasn't an enjoyable experience for me. The teachers taught from text books that stressed literary Chinese. We students wanted to learn to speak Cantonese, the commonly spoken dialect in Hawai'i. Although I didn't care for the classroom agenda, I did meet a lifelong friend, Jackie Lee, and we had lots of fun at recess. We often went to the nearby crack-seed store to buy a little bag of red ginger for a nickel. How we loved snacking on it, and after we had eaten the last little piece, we licked the inside of the bag.

Every Friday, Father came to town to pick up provisions for the store. He also picked us up so that our family would be together for the weekend. The steep, winding ride down the old Pali Road to "the other side" was scenic and circuitous and it often scared me, especially if it was foggy. I would hide under the dashboard and close my eyes.

Once in Kailua, we stocked shelves, cleaned the market, and helped customers find items. Those were the days when groceries were delivered to homes. In Lanikai, most of the homes were fancy houses fronting the wide, yellow, sandy beach. Some of us rode with the delivery person to these luxurious homes and helped cart boxes and bags of groceries through unlocked kitchen doors. Often there would be no one home, so we put whatever needed to be kept cold in the refrigerator so it wouldn't spoil. The other items we left neatly on the counters, and then we would be on our way to the next place.

In Lanikai, many of the elegant homes were rented to famous, and not-so-famous, wealthy people. I remember Shirley Temple, Rochelle Hudson, and Jeanette McDonald. On one occasion, Shirley Temple's bodyguard came to our store to recruit young folks for a softball game with Shirley. It didn't take much time to find enough players. We had such a great time and were very impressed by how modest Shirley was. She was chunky at the time, and wanted to come off as a tomboy. After we finished our game, we were treated to pineapple juice and little animal crackers, and shown their lovely beach. What a memorable experience!

In one corner of our market was a tiny Post Office; Mother was the Postmistress. I learned to sell stamps, sort mail, put it in individual mail cubicles, weigh parcels for postage, and stamp outgoing envelopes. The pigeon-hole size mailboxes for individuals were accessible from the outside so customers could get their mail at any time. The annoying part of having a Post Office in the store was that its hours differed from that of the market; and customers often hassled us for service after the Post Office had closed.

By the time I was ready for seventh grade, my father had a house built on upper Liliha Street, and purchased a drug store in downtown Honolulu on the corner of Bethel and Hotel Streets. In those days, you didn't need to know anything about the pharmacy business to own a drug store. You just read the label and sold the requested item. Mother ran the Lanikai market and father operated the drug store.

The store was just a short distance from Chinese School so each school day I helped out in the store afterwards. One day I was reading an English novel tucked inside a large Chinese text book, something I wasn't supposed to do. I was so absorbed in it that I didn't realize the teacher had come up beside me. Then suddenly, I felt a stinging whack from a bamboo wand on my back. I was so startled and humiliated that all I could do was calmly gather up my books, put them in my tote bag, and leave the classroom. When I showed up earlier than expected at Dad's store, he asked why I had been dismissed so early. I told him what had happened and that I never wanted that teacher to hit me again. My father never physically hit any of us, so no other person was going to do this either. That was the end of my Chinese classes. About the only thing I learned was how to write my name in Chinese and how to use brushes to write Chinese words in calligraphy, something I really enjoyed.

By then, I was attending Robert Louis Stevenson, the English Standard intermediate school, which was quite a distance from our home, so I rode the bus to and from school.

December 7th, 1941, was a sorrowful and dramatic day in our lives as the bombs rained down. I remember vividly that Sunday when we heard the news on the radio at our market in Lanikai. Everyone at the market, including military personnel, had a look of total disbelief on their faces…many had expressions of outright fear. I don't know what possessed me, but I went outside to scan the skies. Suddenly I saw a small airplane with the Japanese logo of a big red sun under its wings. The pilot was flying so low I could see his eyeballs! He was moving from Mōkapu towards Kāne'ohe, and to this day, I don't understand why he didn't shoot me.

After World War II broke out, people built bomb shelters in their back yards for refuge in case of a possible attack. I remember being in the same typing class as my brother Charlie at Stevenson. We sat in alphabetical order and when he was called upon to tell where he would go in case of a bomb alert, he gave the address of our grandmother, who lived within easy walking distance of the school. When it was my turn to tell where I would go, the teacher realized we were heading for the same address and that we were siblings. She bolted out of the classroom to let the principal know because Charlie had a reputation as a real troublemaker, and I was the honored office monitor.

One day there was a bomb alert so we all headed off to our bomb shelters. I remember cajoling Grandma into hurrying to the shelter. She was a woman with bound feet, a status symbol in China, so she was slow and wobbly, and she also insisted on taking lots of worldly goods with her. We never made it to the shelter because the all-clear siren sounded before we arrived. It was still a scary time for us.

War also brought early curfew; we had to be in by 6:00 pm or whenever it got dark. We had black-out curtains over all the windows so no night light would be visible to aid enemy planes. We carried gas masks wherever we went, and gas, sugar, shoes, and many other items were rationed "for the duration."

By the time I entered high school at Roosevelt, my father had sold the drug store and acquired a jewelry store. Dad and I manned the store, and when I wasn't in school, I was the only one watching the goods. My salary was enough to cover my needs. We also sold Hawaiian souvenirs, including fancy embroidered pillow covers, pennants, and hula dolls. These were popular items with the service men who were sent to Hawai'i by the thousands and were based at Pearl Harbor, Hickam Field, or the Marine base at Mōkapu, on the windward side. Because of my after-school job, I had no time to go to football games or take part in other after-school activities, which I really missed.

At Roosevelt, I met June Kau, who was a year younger than I, but we hit it off so well that we even had dresses made alike and loved   being "twins." I remember mentioning to June one day that I was going to wash my hair. Mother overheard me and said it was not a good day to wash one's hair according to her religion. As I had never been exposed to her religion, which was Buddhism, I sneakily told June that we should go to her house to wash my hair.

My most vivid memory of the staff at Roosevelt was Mrs. Nicholson, the acting principal, who took over from Mr. Spencer. She took a liking to me and had me work in the school office each Monday when the other students went off to work in the pineapple fields. I never saw the fields, but heard funny stories about them. By this time I had met my future husband, Bunny Chang, whose birth certificate read Yew Bun Chang. We were Roosevelt classmates and enjoyed each other's company. After school, we often went to downtown Honolulu with other classmates for hot fudge sundaes or *saimin* drenched in soy sauce. In those days, there were many mom-and-pop *saimin* stands and a bowl cost very little money. Then I had to leave to go to work.

During my junior year at Roosevelt, my father was elected as a delegate to the Kuomintang political party in China, representing Hawai'i. He flew to Chungking, China, and during the course of his stay, met Madame Chiang Kai-shek. She persuaded him to send his daughter to her alma mater, Wellesley, a very fine girls' college near Boston, Massachusetts. Because of this, I had no choice but to apply to Wellesley. When I was accepted, everyone breathed a great sigh of relief. My parents were thrilled!

School at Roosevelt was held for only half a day and there were no phys-ed classes as the Navy had taken over part of the school, including the gym and the football field. Nevertheless, I managed to graduate, and in retrospect, regard it as a very good time in my life.

Memories of graduation are vague as I was busy preparing for my first trip to the mainland, and securing permission to travel, another wartime restriction. But I still keep my diploma from Roosevelt as a special memento.

On V J Day, when the war in the Pacific was finally over, I was aboard the S. S. Matsonia, one of Matson Lines' beautiful ocean liners-turned-troop-ship, headed for Wellesley. Along with the hundreds of other passengers, I danced and jumped with joy to think that the war was over and peace was finally restored.

After two years at Wellesley, I wanted to be closer to my boy friend, Bunny Chang, who was attending Stanford, so I transferred there for my junior year. Since my sister, Jenny, was also there, we roomed together. After we graduated from college, Bunny and I married and had two daughters. We decided to remain on the mainland and lived in Hayward, California, for forty-four years. I taught school for twenty years. We now have two grandchildren, and both Bun and I are retired. A few years ago we moved to a retirement home in Union City.

Teddy posing in backyard

Delegates to the Kuomintang political party in China. Center front is Chiang Kai Shek. Father to his left.

JAMES MACKLIN HILL, JR.

It was late Saturday afternoon, March 5, 1960, when my new wife (of about eight hours) and I drove into Kaunakakai from the Moloka'i Airport and stopped at a little grocery store to buy some milk before heading east to the Wills' cottage at Kamalō for our honeymoon. The elderly proprietor allowed as how he had no milk, and that there would be no milk until the next week. He kept staring at me, then took a closer look, peered into my face, pointed his finger and exclaimed, "You're Jim Hill's boy! Wait a minute!" He disappeared into the back of the store and returned with a carton of milk from his own refrigerator. He had not seen me since I was a kid some twenty years ago.

This was the Moloka'i environment in which I was reared. Kaunakakai was a one-street town…the only town on the island. The whole island was one big neighborhood; everyone knew everyone else..... as well as everyone else's business.

My dad, James Macklin Hill, was born in McVeytown, Pennsylvania, in 1899. During World War I, he served in the U.S. Army and was stationed in Hawai'i. After his discharge in1918, he attended business school and got a degree in accounting. After working for a few years, he decided to take a vacation in Hawai'i, and on a side trip to Moloka'i, he met his future wife, Eva McCorristan Dunn. He remained on Moloka'i where they dated for about two years before marrying in 1925. He got a job as Office Manager for Moloka'i Ranch; he was also head of the bank and Post Office in Kaunakakai.

My mom, Eva McCorriston Dunn, who was born in 1901, was one of seven girls and twin boys descended from an old Moloka'i family. All the children attended a small Catholic school with just one classroom, and two nuns taught all the grades from first through twelfth. She grew up in a small house with no electricity. They were a very musical family and entertained themselves playing guitar and 'ukulele with everyone singing along.

The original McCorristons were two brothers who came to O'ahu in 1863 from Derry, Ireland. In 1873 they moved to Moloka'i where they started a sugar plantation at Kamalō. The plantation burned down not long after, and the brothers went into ranching. Several of the Aunties told us we were part Hawaiian but we could never prove it.

After graduation, Mother went to business school in Honolulu and eventually became Moloka'i County Library's head librarian. One of my Aunts was a Moloka'i school teacher, who for many years, every Monday rode horseback over the Kamalō mountains into one of the remote valleys. I seem to remember it was either Waikolu or Pelekunu Valley, where many

Hawaiians grew taro. Due to the great distance, she stayed there during the week, boarding with a family, and rode back out on Friday.

Moloka'i Ranch, where my father worked, was the main income producer on the island. Its origins start with Kamehameha V who gained title to the land in 1863. After his death, the title passed to Princess Ruth, and eventually to Bernice Pauahi. The land then became part of the Bishop Estate and Kamehameha Schools. In 1897, a group of Honolulu businessmen purchased 70,000 acres from the Trustees and leased another 30,000 acres from the Hawaiian government, establishing Moloka'i Ranch. In the early 1900's the land was purchased by Charles M. Cooke, and managed by his son, George P. Cooke. They raised cattle, sweet potatoes, wheat crops and honey. The ranch leased out portions of the land for pineapple cultivation, providing much needed employment for island residents. The ranch provided my parents with a lovely home that came with maid and yard service. They were included in the social activities on the ranch which was located in Kualapu'u, mauka of Kaunakakai. Each year they traveled by steamship to the mainland to visit my paternal grandparents.

There was no hospital on the Island of Moloka'i when I was born in 1926. A few months before my birth, my mother climbed aboard an inter-island ferry and bounced across the channel to Maui to stay with relatives until July 23 when I made my appearance at Lahainaluna Hospital. Within a month or so, we were back at the Ranch. My sister, Sallie, came along ten years later. I wasn't thrilled at having competition for my parents' attention, but I remember trying to be patient as she tagged along, following me everywhere. She says that I taught her to swim and played with her when she was small. I used to take her for rides on the handlebars of my bike. There weren't many smooth roads up *mauka*, so they must have been pretty bumpy

It was really great growing up on Molokai. It was a carefree life; I could ride horses, and run barefoot on the Ranch. George and Sophie Cooke maintained a gracious, and sophisticated lifestyle, unlike my own family, and because of them, I was exposed to a more refined way of life. I was a real *kua'aina*, and the Cookes' were a great influence on me. They welcomed any and all to their home; especially providing a beautiful R&R setting for servicemen during World War II. In the Cooke's huge plantation-style home was a lava rock fireplace that was big enough to walk into. Sometime in the 1950s, they moved into a cottage nearby and the house was given to Queens Hospital, but nothing was ever done with it. In 1966, when the home burned down, the fireplace was the only thing left standing.

When we were really young, my parents told us lots of spooky ghost stories as our family drove from Kaunakakai through Maunawainui Gulch on the way back to the Ranch. The stories were scary, and I crouched down in the back seat to hide until we were past the Gulch.

There was a nine-hole golf course nearby, and when I was big enough to carry a golf bag, I was allowed to caddie for important guests of the Ranch. This launched my lifelong interest in golf. The club house was just a small shack, little bigger than an outhouse. When I was around ten or eleven I got a job washing soda bottles for Uncle George Will, a family friend and manager of what was known as Moloka'i Electric Co. and Soda Works.

When I was ready to enter the eighth grade, I was shipped off to Honolulu to board at 'Iolani School, a boy's Episcopal school which was located, at that time, on Judd Street in Nu'uanu Valley. My parents decided that I needed to learn "proper English" some place other than Moloka'i. Being away from home, and adjusting to a strict routine was kind of hard, but there were plenty of good times; I learned some manners and it prepared me for my high school years. Everyone at the school was friendly so I didn't have a difficult time fitting in. I really don't have many memories of my time at 'Iolani; my friends and I thought it was hilarious when the dining room teacher reminded us frequently to "eat every carrot and pea on your plate!" The other memory I have is when the war came.

On Sunday morning, December 7, 1941, Chapel was cancelled but we were not given a reason. It was most unusual, and when we heard a lot of airplanes flying overhead, a bunch of us went up on the Chapel roof to watch them. We noticed funny, round, red markings under the wings as they flew around and around. I don't remember hearing the bombs, but we could see smoke, and like most everyone else, we assumed it was one of the usual routine military exercises. A little later, we got official word that the Japanese had attacked Pearl Harbor.

There was an immediate curfew, black-out, and martial law was established throughout all the islands. School were closed, but boarders at 'Iolani who were from outside islands remained at the school until transportation could be arranged to take us back to our respective islands. While waiting for a ship to Moloka'i, along with some other boys, I took coffee to the gravediggers at one of the nearby cemeteries.

When I got back to the Ranch, I found our family's house crowded with friends from Kaunakakai and other areas along the shore line; everyone was afraid that there was going to be an enemy invasion throughout the islands and they wanted to get as far away from the coast as possible. Somehow, my parents were able to feed all those folks and find places for them to sleep. I don't remember how long they stayed, or when they went back down to their homes, but it seemed like a very long time.

When schools reopened five months later, I was sent back to Honolulu, but not to 'Iolani. The school had closed for the duration of the war because so many of the students and teachers had gone into the Armed Forces. That's when I started high school at Roosevelt. Until my parents moved to O'ahu, I stayed with my Auntie at her house on Bingham Street near Kapi'olani Hospital. It stood in the middle of what is now the Lunalilo Freeway, just before the Punahou overpass.

In 1943, my parents decided to move to Honolulu. They wanted Sallie to go to better school, and also to be closer to me. Mr. Cooke was not happy with my father leaving and their relationship was strained. As a result, Dad had a hard time finding a job in Honolulu as people were afraid of offending Mr. Cooke by hiring him. Eventually, he got a job with an accounting firm and they bought a small home in Mānoa Valley.

The war, due to curfews and blackouts, curtailed many of our high school activities; but still, it was great fun. The school was surrounded by barbed wire and the Navy had possession of our gym; there were even some sailors in our classes.

In my first year, I tried out for cheerleader, and as I was only a sophomore, I felt honored to be chosen, along with Bill Patton, Bob Beane, and Zelma Zatz, all upperclassmen. After the football games, we all partied as much as possible; somehow I got average grades, then partied some more with the gang. It was important to be an "in" kid, and I thought it was pretty neat to be a member of what was known as the "Famous 5"; some of my best buddies were Tex Hays, Dick Beers, Emmett Hazlett and Warren Gunderson, who became life-long friends. We all hung out on "The Patio," a large, walled-in area in front of the school where they held noon-time or after-school dances on occasion. Sometimes we went down to sit under the beautiful Chinese Banyan tree and played *kamau*, a simple form of bridge. Rumor has it that I occasionally, with several other *kolohe* kids, climbed high up in the branches to sneak a smoke. I don't think we ever got caught, but I would never admit it

As a junior, I was again chosen to be a cheer leader, along with George Hickey, Blondie Boyd, and Frieda Gerlach. After the games, we frequently got together at Blondie's house on

Lusitana Street. She really knew how to put on a party! There were always guys with guitars and 'ukulele singing Hawaiian music, and *Lei Ana Ika* verses that were so popular. They were silly songs about people, places and events and new ones appeared on the campus everyday. We often went to Kailua Beach Park and partied there under the coconut and ironwood trees. On weekends, we sometimes went body surfing at Makapu'u Beach, or to the matinee at the Waikīkī Theater.

During the war years, all high school students were required either to work in the pineapple fields, or the cannery. Most of my friends rode in the back of a truck out to the fields to pick pineapples one day a week. I don't know how Ī got the job, but I worked at Honolulu Harbor hauling crates of pineapples off the plantation trains for shipment to the mainland and elsewhere. This was really hard work for a skinny kid with no muscles, and that hard labor convinced me that either college or the military was a better life than manual labor for the rest of my days.

Throughout high school, I wasn't a particularly good student, probably because I was so involved in partying and having fun, but I did join the Latin Club after studying Latin under Mrs. Gill, the Science Club, and the Pep Rally Committee, which helped to organize the popular pep rallies held in the school auditorium the day before the football games. My favorite teacher at Roosevelt was Miss Virginia McBride, who taught junior English. Although she was very strict, she had a special way of teaching that really inspired me. Our principal, Robert Spencer, was a large, heavy man with a balding head; later Mrs. Nicolson became acting principal when he took a leave of abscence for the duration of the war. In my junior year, our team won the Interscholastic Football Championship when the top football players from 'Iolani transferred to Roosevelt.

Beating Punahou, our biggest rival, was an occasion to gloat over, and it was a tradition for Roosevelt students to sneak over at night and paint the dome on the Punahou campus red and gold, Roosevelt colors; they would paint our dome Punahou colors, yellow and blue. We were rivals, but friendly ones, and often we attended their post-game parties and they came to ours as well.

Graduation came all too quickly. At the graduation ceremony, held in the Roosevelt Auditorium, we marched onto the stage to receive our diplomas and soon found ourselves draped in lei from friends and relatives. Afterwards, we attended a party held at a nightclub to celebrate. It was a great evening and a fitting climax to our school years. Fortunately, the war was winding down and the future looked bright. I knew I would soon be joining the Army and looked forward to it with great anticipation.

Soon after graduation, I served two years in the Army, most of the time in Germany. After my discharge, I attended the University of Oregon, graduating in 1951 when I was hired by Pan American World Airways. After living in San Francisco for several years, I came home on vacation one year and I decided I didn't want to go back to the mainland. Luckily, I was able to get a transfer and spent a total of 22 years with the airline. In 1958 I met Sarah "Sally" Davis on a triple blind date. We were married in 1960. We have two sons and three grandchildren.

Hill family on Moloka'i

Mack Hill as cheerleader

YVONNE NEELY ARMITAGE HODGINS

How and why I grew up in Hawai'i was truly a stroke of luck as my four grandparents came from the four corners of the earth...Nova Scotia, the Azores, French-speaking Canada, and England.

My paternal grandparents met on a ship traveling from Honolulu to Australia in the late 1890s. My grandmother, who came from the Azores, was a governess for the children of one of the early missionary families. My grandfather, a mate on the ship, and originally from Nova Scotia, met, and fell in with love with her. After the ship returned to Honolulu, they married and he later left the ship and became a member of the Royal Guard that patrolled 'Iolani Palace during the latter days of the monarchy; after the overthrow, he worked in the customs office. Their three children were my father, Arthur, born in 1899, the oldest, and two younger girls.

On my mother's side, her maternal ancestors crossed the border from Canada and settled in Fon du Lac, Wisconsin. Her father's ancestors, originally from England, had immigrated to the United States and lived in upstate New York. By coincidence, a relative of my mother, Rev. Heman Humphrey, a former president of Amherst College in Massachusetts, ordained the first group of missionaries who came to Hawai'i in 1820.

After her husband passed away, left with seven small children, my grandmother moved from Wisconsin to southern California, a daring move at the time, especially since she had no relatives there that we know of. Happily, all the children turned out well; Mother went to nursing school; one of her brothers became a set designer for movies, and a well-known sculptor. He designed religious sculptures for many of the Catholic churches and schools in greater Los Angeles and also entered a world-wide contest to design a plaque for Sarah Bernhardt's grave in Paris... and won!

Mother entered the nursing program at Methodist Hospital in Los Angeles and became a registered nurse. After graduating, she worked her way up to chief nurse in the operating room but eventually got burned out and took a job as a private duty nurse for the terminally ill wife of a wealthy Boston lawyer. After her patient's death, she was gifted with a considerable amount of money. With this stipend, she and a fellow nurse decided to see the world and sailed on the S.S. Calawai to Honolulu. They intended to stay in the islands for a few months before continuing to the Orient.

While they were in Honolulu, a typhoid epidemic broke out. The ladies cancelled their travel plans and answered a plea for medical personnel having experience with tracheotomy patients. They bought white uniforms, white shoes, white socks, and turned themselves in to Queen's Hospital. They never did get to the Orient.

After the epidemic, both ladies decided to stay in Hawai'i and mother took a job as chief nurse at 'Ewa Plantation Hospital. There she met my father who worked for the plantation, and they were married at Watertown, where Pearl City is now. They had a garden wedding on December 31, 1925, with all her fellow nurses in attendance, and my father's family as well.

When mother became pregnant for the first time, complications developed and my parents temporarily moved to California to be near mother's family. I was born there on February 11, 1927. We returned to Honolulu when I was eleven months old. My brother, Arthur Dwight Neely, was born two years later in Honolulu. During my early years we lived in Kaimuki where I started school at Ali'iolani.

When my father got a job as mill engineer at Līhu'e Plantation, we moved to Kaua'i. The plantation provided us with a nice house on Rice Street, the main thoroughfare of Līhu'e, where I met a new friend and playmate, Jane Frizelle, whose father was principal of Kaua'i High School. I spent a lot of time at her home and one day, when we got bored, we climbed one of the "Portagee" plum trees along the road, and after gathering a large number of the soft, purple, staining berries, pelted the cars passing below us. Someone must have turned us in because not long after, a policeman in his heavy wool, olive-drab uniform, arrived; he ordered us out of the tree and escorted us back to Jane's house. I don't remember what our punishment was but I don't think it was too severe as, once the officer left, Mrs. Frizelle appeared to be quite amused by the incident.

Another day we decided to make jam out of "Portagee" plums, but that didn't turn out too well either. We ended up making a mess of Mrs. Frizelle's kitchen and perm- anently staining her drip pans and stove burners. I took home a jar to my mother but she bent her silver spoon in half trying to get the dense, dark stuff out of the jar. I don't think I had much to do with "Portagee" plums after that.

When September came, I entered Līhu'e Grammar School where most of the plantation children went. After two years in Līhu'e, my father took a job teaching vocational shop to high school drop-outs and parolees in Kalaheo, a small town on Kaua'i on the way to Waimea and Kekaha. There I attended Kalaheo Grammar School. We were only there for one year, but the thing I remember most was the day a huge tent appeared in the pasture next to our house. It was occupied by a band of Romanian Gypsies. Everyone in the neighborhood was warned to keep their doors locked. We were all fascinated by them and their colorful garb.

As you can see, we did a lot of moving, and after just one year at Kalaheo, we moved back to Līhu'e, but this time to a house next to the plantation store. It was then that I entered fourth grade. What a wonderful experience it was, thanks to my teacher, Miss Grace Hegge, an exchange teacher from Chambersberg, Pennsylvania. We all loved her teaching methods as she truly broadened our horizons. In geography and history, in particular, she made foreign places seem so real and the historic figures were like real people.

Our principal, Miss Edith Croller, was also very creative and innovative. After lunch every Friday, all eight grades would meet in the auditorium, boys on the left, girls on the right, to sing from song books she provided. Wonderful American songs like My Old Kentucky Home, Flow Gently Sweet Afton, Old Black Joe, and many others. We had a great time. Every Halloween she came to school in a witch's costume with a tall conical hat, a long pointed nose, carrying a broom stick. She visited every single class on the campus, causing the kids to shriek and holler.

If you were naughty, you were put on the demerit list, and to work them off you were required to go out in the vast playground to gather *hilahila* plants. With a pail and weeder you dug up the thorny plants until the pail was full. But even that was better than detention.

And then we moved again, this time to Kealia, which was situated on a hill about twenty miles north of Līhuʻe on the way to Hanalei. The plantation store and other shops were located at the bottom of the hill, and the plantation camps, separated into Japanese and Filipino camps, were located above. Our house was in between. There was a lot of segregation on the plantations, which at the time, we simply took for granted. At Kealia Plantation, when we went to the movies, (there was just one small theater in the town) we *haoles* sat in large wicker chairs on a platform just below the projection room; the regular seats were assigned to the other plantation workers.

As there was no school in Kealia, I continued to attend Līhuʻe Grammar School, getting there and home each day via a "sampan taxi," an open, rebuilt sedan with bench-like seats along the back and both sides. Our driver, Mrs. Yoshida, appeared every day dressed in khaki pants, a blue work shirt, *palaka* jacket, big white gardening gloves with blue cuffs, and a pith helmet. She was a treasure!

In June of 1941 we graduated from the eighth grade at Līhuʻe Grammar and entered Kauaʻi High School in Līhuʻe in September. The adjustment was easy as my classmates were pretty much the same, and life was pretty uneventful until that day in early December when our lives were turned upside down.

December 7ᵗʰ, 1941, started out as just another lazy Sunday. After breakfast I was listening to big band music on the radio. Suddenly the announcer broke in with the news that the Japanese were bombing Pearl Harbor. I rushed out to my father's shop in the shed in the backyard yelling, "Daddy, the man on the radio said that the Japanese are bombing Pearl Harbor!" "Its just war games," he replied, so I went back to listen to the music, but there was none. Just the droning voice of the announcer repeating his message: "The Japanese are bombing Pearl Harbor. Everybody take cover." Again I ran to my father, but again he refused to even consider the possibility. In my third attempt, I told him that the station had played the Star Spangled Banner and then went off the air. Finally he reconsidered.

A lieutenant in the B.M.T.C (Business Men's Training Corps), he made a few brief phone calls, put on his uniform, strapped his revolver to his waist, and left. We didn't see him for three days. My mother, brother, and I spent a frightening and anxious night alone. The next day President Roosevelt declared war against Japan. When my father returned, he told us that in order to prevent any landing on the island by enemy planes, he had rounded up his men and all the plowing equipment from the plantation and plowed up all the flat land that could be used for landing.

In the following days, we learned that the army had taken over Kauai High School for a field hospital. We were finger-printed and issued I.D. cards and gas masks. All schools were closed and supplies in the plantation store grew scantier every day. Fortunately, we had a vegetable garden in our back yard so we had an ample supply of fresh carrots, cabbage, bell peppers and broccoli. The plantation sent crews to dig bomb shelters in the yards of all the plantation houses. Air Raid Wardens patrolled the neighborhoods at night and curfew and blackout were strictly enforced. Rationing cards were issued for such items as liquor and gasoline; mail was censored.

Later in December, a Japanese submarine came into Nawiliwili Harbor in an attempt to blow up the gasoline tank. It set off a flare to illuminate the tank, but it turned into a fiasco when they mistook the molasses tank for the gas tank and the flare drifted into an adjacent cane field. The cane field caught on fire but the fire trucks and police cars responding to the dilemma couldn't make any headway as the roads were covered with spilled molasses, causing them to slip and slide all over. Late that night, my father went off to direct his men in an emergency operation at the harbor, but since he had forgotten to put his dentures in, his speech was so incoherent that the men couldn't understand a word he said.

With everyone focused on the attack, we forgot all about Christmas which was just around the corner. The bountiful supply of fragrant Douglas fir trees that were always shipped from the Pacific Northwest didn't arrive, so we improvised with a large guava tree branch which we decorated with ornaments, lights and all the trimmings. It was a quiet Christmas compared to our usual yuletide celebration, but it was just one of many of our usual customs that disappeared "for the duration."

Soon Army troops began to arrive by the boat-load to set up Field and Coast Artillery Stations around the Island. Since there were no military bases on Kaua'i before the war, they were billeted in schools and public and private buildings of all kinds. Armed soldiers patrolled the perimeter of Kaua'i High School twenty-four hours a day. My mother turned our dining room into a Red Cross bandage center where people from the neighborhood, both male and female, gathered to do their part for the war effort. Because of the food shortage, mother did a lot of improvising; she made mock apple pie out of Ritz crackers, butter from coconut milk, and cooked endless, dreary, meatless meals. She also cooked many batches of cookies for the soldiers. Some she passed out to the patrols that marched past our house; my brother, on his bicycle, delivered others to the men in the fox holes down on the coast.

Jane and I got to know a couple of the soldiers named Frank and Ernest. We asked Mrs. Frizelle if we could invite them over for dinner some evening and she agreed. It turned out the boys weren't too bright and after they left, Mr. Frizelle renamed them "Null" and "Void."

Because the high school was not available for classes, the grammar school was utilized for both elementary and upper classes. The lower classes attended school from 7:00 a.m. until noon. High school was held from 1:00 p.m. to 5:00 p.m. I was pretty tall for my age, and what a time I had trying to squeeze into one of those little nailed-down desks. So imagine what the big, brawny football players went through! But somehow we all managed.

When school was over in June, my parents decided to send me to the mainland to live with my mother's spinster sister in Highland Park, California. Many families had already moved away, others sent their children, and in some cases, just the girls. It was a long difficult process to get permission to travel and I was put on a waiting list, not knowing when I would be called. Finally the word arrived and my father drove me the fifty miles from Kealia to 'Ele'ele where I met my friend Jane Frizelle who was being sent to Milwaukee to live with relatives. There we boarded a small, blacked-out propeller plane for Honolulu to await a ship that would take us to the west coast. I stayed with a family friend until the word came that the ship was ready for boarding.

Finally the call came and I was delivered to the pier where the ship was waiting. By coincidence, I met up with my friend Jane and we traveled on the USS President Johnson as part of a convoy accompanying a hospital ship, the USS Henderson. We didn't have a stateroom, but slept in the main salon which was decorated with cupids, clouds, birds, and flowers painted on the ceiling, with lots of gilt everywhere. The large room was filled with three-tiered bunk beds; I got a top one. The lower decks were filled with troops being sent to the mainland for training, but we were not allowed to mingle with them. Jane and I spent our time reading to little children, playing cards, and walking the decks.

Following a zig-zag course, it took ten days to reach San Francisco. Jane and I parted at the dock on arrival, and there I was, a scared, fifteen year old from a small island alone in a big city. All I had was my grandmother's address, but somehow I managed to get a taxi to take me to her apartment. After a few days I got on a train that took me to Burbank where my Aunt Belle greeted me at the station. From there we drove to Highland Park where she lived in a small apartment, and in the fall, I began my sophomore year at Benjamin Franklin Senior High. I expected to feel like an outsider but it turned out that there were several other students whose families had recently moved to California to take jobs connected with the war effort. So it was easy to make friends. The school offered dancing instruction every morning before class began, and this was another way to get acquainted with fellow students.

If your grades were good, the school would let you off early to work if you had a part time job. I applied for a social security card and was hired by S. H. Kress and Company as a sales clerk. I also had a second job with the May Company in downtown Los Angeles where I sold ladies' ready-to-wear in their basement shop, which was not nearly as classy as the rest of the store. All my clients were "Rosie the Riveter" types, wearing hard-toed boots, overalls, with their hair tied up in bandanas. They tried on, and invariably bought, the frilliest dresses imaginable.

While I was in California, my parents moved back to Oʻahu, so I never returned to Kauaʻi to live. At the end of the school year, I bade a tearful farewell to my new friends but kept in touch with many of them for years after. It was the summer of 1943 and this time it was left to me to go through the process of getting permission to travel. After corresponding with the Commandant of the 14th Naval District, pleading my case, I was advised to have a whole series of shots, be packed, and await a phone call announcing the ship's departure. This time I returned on the Matson ship, S.S. Matsonia, the former luxury-liner-turned-troop-ship. I was assigned to a small stateroom with others who were young women coming to Honolulu to take jobs already secured with the military government. The voyage was pretty much a repeat of the one a year earlier; we traveled in a convoy and whiled away the time as best we could.

My father had bought a house in Woodlawn, a new subdivision on the upper slopes of Mānoa Valley. Not far below us was the Mānoa Chinese Cemetery. One day I got off the bus there, went in, and took an orange from someone's grave before walking the rest of the way home. My mother was horrified and wanted me to take it back but I begged her to let me keep it as I hadn't tasted a fresh orange in months and months. She reluctantly let me, but made me promise never to do it again.

Funeral processions to the Chinese Cemetery traveled along East Mānoa Road and were quite fascinating to behold. Long lines of people, including professional mourners dressed in white robes, marched along, their wailing voices so loud they could be heard from one side of the valley to the other. Thin strips of tissue-like paper punched with hundreds of little holes were tossed about. It was said that evil spirits had to pass through every single hole to reach the spirit of the deceased. What we really looked for were the little red folded papers containing nickels and dimes that were tossed out of the windows of the cars. Drums and horns followed the hearse which usually carried a large, framed photograph of the deceased mounted on the top. After getting accustomed to my new neighborhood, I began to think of school. It was an easy decision to make as Roosevelt, the only English Standard high school on the island, was not too far away, and easily accessed by bus. During the summer, to make up some credits, I attended summer school, which gave me a chance to get acquainted with other students before starting my junior year.

I loved Roosevelt from the beginning. It was designed in a style of Spanish architecture and set on a small hill not far from Punchbowl. I was really impressed with my fellow students who were all so nice, considerate, and easy to make friends with. Much to my surprise, I found one of my fellow students was my old buddy, Jane Frizelle, who traveled all the way from Waialua each day as her father was now principal of Waialua High School.

I joined the choir, which the school was noted for, and our director, Alda Coito Lee, was full of encouragement for everyone. The choir was really good and often asked to put on concerts for the military. We traveled to such places as Schofield Barracks, Pearl Harbor, Hickam Air Base, and the Royal Hawaiian Hotel, which had been taken over by the Navy as a place for R & R (Rest and Recreation) for the submarine troops. The choir was also a great place to make friends.

As part of the war effort, all high school students were required to work in the pineapple fields one day a week. The plantation attire consisted of jeans, long-sleeved *palaka* shirts, sneakers, bandanas which we wore around our necks, heavy gloves, goggles and straw hats with wide brims. We arrived at school before seven in the morning where we proceeded to pile into one of the large trucks with a canvas cover and rows of seats that transported us to the plantations. On the long ride to Wahiawā, we waved at the service men we passed along the way and sang all the latest songs; the popular *"Le Ana Ika"* verses were our favorites.

Life in the fields was very harsh and primitive. There were no shade trees, no comfort stations, water fountains, or any shelter from the elements. Just lots of swirling red dust! Under the watchful eye of an unsmiling *luna*, we spent the day in the hot sun bagging slips, picking pineapples, or pulling weeds. Despite our heavy clothing, we often got scratched by the sharp, pointed leaves. All there was, when we had to "go," was a flimsy, burlap-covered portable *lua*; we had to dig a hole in the center with our hoe.

One day I picked up a burlap bag and slung it over my shoulder. Instantly my face, neck, armpits.... my whole body down to my waist, was on fire. I had disturbed the nest of a swarm of stinging red ants. I screamed and the *lunas* came running. *"Hemo da shirt,"* they yelled, but too embarrassed to undress, I suffered the pain as they did their best to get the nasty little critters off me.

The rest of the week at school, we spent most of our recesses on the large patio in front of the main building, or sat on the grass under the huge Chinese banyan tree playing a simple form of bridge called *kamau*. Afternoon dances were occasionally held on the patio after school because we couldn't go anywhere at night due to the blackout.

After school, we often caught the bus and went downtown where we hung out at Benson Smith Drug Store, sitting around the counter slurping root beer floats and meeting kids from other schools who gathered there too. One of the "fixtures" in the area was a somewhat peculiar woman who we learned was a member of the well-known McInerney family. Dressed entirely in black, she cleaned the ashtrays, mopped up spills, and if you came across her in the ladies' room, she would hand you a paper towel as you finished washing your hands. Mary McInerney patrolled Fort Street, picking up cigarette butts, which she later smoked. She was the only adult that attended the Mickey Mouse Club at the Princess Theater on Saturday morning.

We loved rainy, muddy days. When the clouds burst, we would frantically look for someone with a car to drive us up to Tantalus, an extinct cinder cone on the southern Koʻolau Range, to go *ti* leaf sliding. We sloshed up the hillside, grabbed a *ti* leaf plant, sat on the leaves while holding the ends of the stems in our hands in front of us, and slid down the slippery slope while gazing into verdant Mānoa Valley. We'd also go up to Tantalus to pick yellow ginger blossoms that grew wild over the hillside and make lei to wear to the football games. After the game we'd rush out on the field to give the lei and a big smooch to our favorite football player.

Another favorite pastime was going up to Nuʻuanu Valley to swim at Jackass Ginger, a delightful, clear pool at the bottom of a waterfall. It was reached by the Judd trail that zigzagged back and forth over Nuʻuanu stream, surrounded by *ti* and wild ginger blossoms. There was a type of ginger we called "shampoo ginger" that we would break off and use to whack each other over the head.

Needless to say, the few people that owned a car were very much in demand.

Swimming and body-surfing at places like Makapuʻu and Sandy Beach were popular weekend activities, as was going to the Saturday matinee at the Waikīkī Theater, across the street from the Outrigger Canoe Club where many of us hung out whether we were members or not. At the theater, the head usherette stood rigidly in the center of the hall directing the patrons to the right or left. Dressed in white slacks and shirt, with a bright yellow feather cape across her shoulders, she was a most impressive figure. The theater itself was a masterpiece of real-looking tropical foliage and flowers. White clouds drifted across the velvet blue sky as Edwin Sawtelle played the pipe organ; the sides of the theater were lined with life-like coconut trees, bougainvillea, and night blooming cereus.

If you forgot your shoes, a requirement of the theater, you would wait for a friend to go in and then toss the footwear out the side door of the theater where you would be aiting. Several people sometimes got in the theater on just one pair of shoes. The movie began with the March of Time which brought us up to date on the latest war news, followed by a cartoon featuring Mickey Mouse or Porky Pig. Some of the movies I remember are *Bataan*, which made me cry, *Life Boat* with Tallulah Bankhead, and *The Outlaw* with Jane Russell.

During summer vacation, I got a job at Liberty House, Honolulu's only upscale department store. All the salesladies were required to wear white dresses in the spring and summer, and black in the fall and winter. Mrs. French, the head floor lady, stood outside the employee entrance every morning to inspect everyone as they arrived for work, even checking to make sure the seams in their rayon hose were straight. (Nylon stockings were one of the casualties of the war.) Many of my customers in the cosmetic department were "madams" from the brothels on Hotel Street.

My two years at Roosevelt passed quickly, and before I knew it, we were planning graduation and thinking about what we were going to do afterward. The ceremony took place in the school auditorium followed by a banquet at Hawaiian Town in Moʻiliʻili. Blackout was still in effect so we had to get blackout passes and submit the name of our date in advance so I was disappointed when the fellow I had asked dropped out at the last minute. An old friend came through and we were able to get the name changed just in time. It was a great evening... dancing to Hawaiian music, eating *laulau* and *poi*, enjoying the scent of *pikake* and ginger blossoms that permeated the room. It was the end of a wonderful two years that I will always treasure. Some classmates I never saw again. Others are still a part of my life. Perhaps because of the war and the fact that so many families had been disrupted by it, there was a special bonding among us that exists to this day.

With high school behind me, I went to work at Hawaiian Electric Company as a Personnel Clerk, in charge of hiring and firing employees. In 1950 I married John Armitage and built a lovely home in Nuʻuanu. We had two children, Lorna and Paul, and two grandchildren. At the age of 50 I divorced John and spent the next ten years living in a condominium in downtown

Honolulu before moving to Volcano on the Big Island, buying land, building a house, and starting new life. After moving back to O'ahu in 1993, I got a call from a widowed Volcano neighbor, Stanley Hodgins, and we hit it off. At the age of 66, I became a bride for the second time. Stanley passed away in 2006.

Parents wedding

Yvonne after Sunday School

DONALD CHING

I was born in 1927 in Hoʻaeʻae, ʻEwa District, Island of Oʻahu, Territory of Hawaii. There were ten children in the family, four boys and six girls. I was number nine, the youngest boy. Mama, Polly Yuke Chin Lee, was born in 1891 in Kaneʻohe. She was of the second generation of her family born in Hawaiʻi, and one of eight children. Her father was a rice planter and also the manager of the Kaneʻohe Rice Mill. Mama had completed the third grade, and with that education, she was our guiding force. She spoke English and Papa did not, so she was the spokesperson in family and business matters. When we asked her, "Ma, can we go?" She would sternly correct us, "May we go?" She worked the crosswords assiduously and  had a tremendous vocabulary. She was adept in different languages, conversing easily with Hawaiians and Japanese. She read the newspapers thoroughly.

Papa, Den Loy Ching, was born in 1876 in Yu Fu, Dung Goon District, Kwangtung, China, about 60 miles northeast of Hong Kong, below Canton. He came to Hawaiʻi at the turn of the century and worked for ʻEwa Plantation for a few years before starting his own rice farm in Hoʻaeʻae. Papa was smart. We all knew that. My older sister, Flossie, used to say that it was too bad he had never learned to speak English... he would have gone a long way. But when you looked at the farm he carved out by himself, you realized that he had indeed come a long, long way from China. The farm layout... banana fields, vegetable plots, rice fields, were all carefully terraced, and the water distribution system he devised took a lot of intelligent engineering and hard work.

Hoʻaeʻae was rural... real country. We didn't have electricity or a telephone, so we used wood from *kiawe* and *haole koa* trees for cooking; we had kerosene lamps, lanterns and an outhouse. We didn't have a car, and our only real access to the outside world, Honolulu, was by train.

Hoʻaeʻae was a village of nine houses strung along the railroad tracks on the shores of West Loch, Pearl Harbor, between Waipahu and Honouliuli. The train ran twice a day from Honolulu to Kahuku. It started out from Iwilei, in Honolulu, passed through Damon Tract, Watertown, Aiea, Pearl City, and then Waipahu. Waipahu was the last stop before the "country." There the train stopped to take on water and the passengers got off to buy goodies.

Hoʻaeʻae was seventeen telephone poles after Apoka, another tiny town along the train tracks where nine families lived; three were farmers, the rest were fishermen, each with his own pier where the sailboats docked.

Papa leased ten acres on a slight slope overlooking West Loch. About three-quarters of it was planted with rice, bananas, and vegetables. Behind the house, was the "forest" with kiawe and *haole koa* trees, then the cane fields. There were several springs which furnished cold, clean, artesian water. Papa sank a barrel into one of them for our "well".

The main house had three small bedrooms, a living room, and a porch which we called the "randa." The kitchen was a separate building with a table and benches, a fireplace for cooking, a place to store the firewood, a food cabinet, and a barrel to keep our bath water. Next to the barrel was a bucket of clean, fresh water for cooking. We bathed in a small, enclosed area, perhaps six by eight feet, with walls about six feet high. When we bathed, we heated water on the fire, mixed it with cold water in a bucket, then scrubbed ourselves with a soapy towel.

The house overlooked West Loch, which was about 100 yards away. There was a small yard, then a vegetable garden where we grew *fu qua, see qua,* tomatoes, eggplant, cucumbers, and rice. There was also a fish pond... then the railroad track and West Loch. Across the Loch we could see some of industrial Pearl Harbor, and far in the distance, above the sugar cane and *kiawe* trees, was Honolulu. We could see the top of Diamond Head, Tantalus, and the Kamehameha Schools auditorium. It was our glimpse of the outside world, a world so far away.

Papa raised rice the way he had learned in China... with hard work and a constant battle with nature. In the early spring he prepared the fields for planting. He would be behind the plow, the water buffalo pulling, and Mama leading the water buffalo, carrying baby sister, Ruth, on her back. After working in the fields all day, she cooked dinner for our large family. We had hired help for the planting and Mama cooked lunch for all of them as well.

After the rice was planted, there was nothing to do for several months. The stalks began to have grains of rice which slowly ripened and started to turn golden-brown. Papa carefully watched his ripening crop, and so did the rice birds. They came, more and more each day, to feast. Papa rigged up cords from the house to the far reaches of the fields. He hung tin cans on the lines, and when the birds came, we would pull on the lines. "Katang, katang, katang." The noise would scare the birds away. But, pretty soon they wised up and sat on the swaying lines, having a good time. A change in tactics was in order. Each of the children was stationed in a different section of the fields. We would yell to chase the birds away. Not "shoo" or "go away," but "heow hett, heow hett, heow hett, hett, hett," just like in China. When we got tired of chasing rice birds, we sneaked through the rice to play cards. When Papa noticed the birds feasting and the quietness in the fields, he came charging through the rice looking for us. We scattered to our appointed posts, and the cries of "heow hett" rang out. After awhile the birds got used to this, so Papa went to his last line of defense. He cleaned his musket... we called it a rice patch gun... poured in the gun powder, cocked the hammer, rushed out into the midst of the feasting birds, shouted a few choice Chinese words and "kapow!" He fired into the air. The frightened birds flew to the trees to watch and wait. Finally, after a few days of "kapow," Papa would put a few kernels of rice into his mouth, chew and pronounce that the rice was ready for harvest After the fields were drained, and the mud was firm enough to walk on, we all helped harvest the rice. It was very hard work.

When the rice weevil and California rice put an end to rice growing in Hawaii, Papa and Mama turned to growing white ginger flowers for the lei sellers. We got up very early in the morning, lantern and bucket on one arm, and picked the buds. We counted fifty, tied them together with banana stalk fiber, and put them in the bucket. The train to Honolulu came by at 6:00 a.m. and every morning there was a frantic rush... Mama wolfing down a boiled egg, gulping instant Postum, and rushing to catch the train which usually waited for her if she was late.

Ginger season lasted from July to Thanksgiving. At the peak, we harvested 11,000 buds a day and got ten cents per hundred, which came to $11.00. This was our main cash crop and it had to support the family for the whole year. The lei sellers only bought on "Boat Days," when the Lurline, Maru ships, or President liners were in port. But we were rich enough that Mama bought cupcakes in Honolulu, probably days old, and we each had one apiece. She bought fruit... grapes, peaches, apricots... probably seconds, but we didn't care, we just gobbled them up.

On days when there was no boat and no market for our ginger buds, we were spared from waking up early in the dark to pick the buds. In the afternoon the fields would be covered with blossoms. The 4:30 p.m. train would stop and the passengers would get off to take pictures. After the train left, we picked all the opened blossoms and threw them away, getting ready for the next morning. When the weather was dry, we watered every bulb in the afternoon so that the next morning's buds would be plump and easy to pick.

There was always something that had to be done. Every weekend we went into the *kiawe* and *haole koa* field to look for dried branches for firewood. Once a year Papa cut down a big *kiawe* tree for our main supply, but every weekend we gathered dry branches to supplement it. On Fridays, we brought out all the lamps and lanterns and cleaned the chimneys, trimmed the wicks, and refilled the kerosene.

Our chores were never-ending. The wooden barrel in the kitchen where we stored our bath water had to be cleaned and filled. Banana stumps had to be peeled and dried for string to tie vegetables and bunches of ginger buds. Sleeves had to be made of newspaper to cover the *fu qua* and *see qua*. Chickens and ducks had to be cared for. Saturday was wash day... we all did our own laundry, and Sunday was for ironing clothes. During the summer, the older sisters sewed our clothes for the next school year.

One of our main jobs during the summer was to clean out the banana patches. We cut off the dried fronds, which we called *keiki*, and hauled away the accumulated stumps to a compost pile. Sometimes we would run into a yellow jacket nest and the bees would come buzzing, looking for someone to sting. We laid low until the bees settled back in their nest. Then Ernest, our older brother, set fire to a roll of newspapers and warily approached the nest, chasing the bees away with smoke. When the nest was cleared, he motioned to me to move in and grab it while he kept the bees at bay. I would sneak in, grab the nest and run. Then we went to the kitchen, stirred up the fire, and roasted the bee's nest after which we all feasted on roasted bee larvae. Good eat!

After we cleared the fields, Papa diverted the running stream to flood the fields. But first, we rounded up all the ducks and put them safely away. The chickens were left to roam. Why the ducks and not the chickens? When the fields were flooded, all kinds of insects and bugs would come out. The chickens would have a field day, running around, pecking away at the feast. Sometimes one of them would catch a mouse. It would try to run away from the pack to enjoy the prize by itself. The rest would give chase, hoping to get a share. Not so ducks. Their bills are not built for pecking. They would scoop up whatever was loose and swallow it. Centipedes swallowed live and whole would sting them in their insides and the ducks would die. That's why we had to lock them up.

Education for their children was very important to Mama and Papa; in China, only the very rich sent their children to school and an entire village would pool their money to send one male child to school to bring honor to the village. Girl babies were an economic liability. Our family was smart... not geniuses, but smart. Each of us, when we hit the third grade, was promoted to the fourth after one semester. All except Edna, that is. Edna leaped from second to fourth grade.

Late one afternoon, we were sitting on our "randa" when a car drove into our neighbor's yard. Two *haole* ladies, wearing hats, got out of the car and headed for our house. We couldn't imagine who they were or why they were here! It turned out that our oldest sister, Laura, was being offered a scholarship to Mid Pacific Institute. It was a momentous decision for Mama and Papa because Laura was expected to go to work (she had just graduated from 8th grade) to help support the family, but she went to MPI, leading the way for three of her younger sisters.

Later, the same scenario was repeated with sister, Florence (Flossie). Only this time there was a sequel; after Flossie graduated from MidPac, the same ladies came to see Mama and Papa. Their message: "Flossie should go to the University of Hawaii." I can still remember my Aunt telling Mama, "faht mung" (crazy). Waste of money. Send her to sewing school." Papa shook his head and told Flossie that if she went, she could not expect any help. Flossie went and six of us brothers and sisters followed.

We grew up with clams and clamming. The clams grew in the mud flats of West Loch, in front of our house. They lived under the mud about a half-inch below the surface. They stuck their siphons up through the mud to feed. At low tide you could see hundreds of little holes in the mud. When we walked on the mud and spotted the holes, we stuck a finger or big spoon under it, and scooped up a clam, and put it in a bucket. When we had a gallon, we took them home for dinner.

Same thing with crabs; all we needed was some string. We would catch our bait (*o'opu* or *pan tat*), and take it in a bucket with a scoop net, down to our pier. Then we tied the cut-up bait to the end of the string with a piece of finger coral from the railroad track. We tossed the weighted bait into the shallow water and tied the loose end to the pier. Pretty soon a crab would come and pull on the bait. We retrieved the line very slowly, and with the bait and crab hanging on, scooped them both up with a net. We caught just enough for the family to eat.

As there were no doctors in our area, to reach one we had to catch the train. Consequently, whatever sicknesses we had, we used folk medicine,... Chinese or Hawaiian. One of the Chinese folk remedies was *fu qua kon*. Mama would slice and dry the *fu qua* and save it for an emergency. When we got sick, a handful of it was simmered with a dried oyster. The ensuing broth was like thick coffee, but when it was brewing, it gave off an awful smell; the taste of it was even worse. Once, sister Edna and I got sick and Mama brewed up a batch of *fu qua kon*. We could smell it cooking and knew what was coming. When it was done, Mama brought a cup and a spoon to us. We both yelled, "Ma, *pau* sick already! No need *fu qua kon*!" Needless to say, Mama made us each swallow a spoonful gave us a dried Chinese date as a reward, and amazingly, we were cured. *Pau* sick! Much later, I asked my doctor about this and he informed me that *fu qua* was a good source of quinine which explains the bitterness. Seems like the old folks knew what they were doing.

Papa was very religious. In his quiet way, he followed his beliefs. He never did anything to harm anybody. Every year, just before New Year's, Papa went to town to buy incense, candles, special foods and firecrackers. On New Year's Eve at about 4:30 p.m., the family gathered in the yard around a food-laden table. There were usually a boiled chicken, and fresh and candied fruit served as food offerings. Papa lit the incense and candles and we all bowed three times before lighting a string of firecrackers. Afterwards we feasted on the offered food, and at midnight Papa set off another string of firecrackers.

Because we lived in the country, everything had to be brought in by train or carried from Waipahu, two-and-a-half miles away. Everything was used over and over... recycled. Our kerosene came in five-gallon cans. When the cans were empty, we cut off the top, made holes in the top edges, and used them for buckets. When the holes wore out, there was another can to take its place and the old one was flattened and used to patch our shingle roof. The roof was just a patchwork of wooden shingles and rusty kerosene cans. Nails were saved, the bent ones straightened. White rice bags were used for clothes. The ashes from our fireplace were used to clean our pots and pans and Chinese bowls.

I started school at August Ahrens School in Waipahu, and remained there through the sixth grade. August Ahrens was originally the school for children of plantation management and supervisors. It later became an English Standard School. It was about two-and-a-half miles from our house, and we walked to and from school every day.

Everything was new and wonderful at school...sometimes puzzling, but wonderful. Our teachers, who came from the Mainland, were determined to make us all "Americans". One of them would tell us how important it was to have a good and proper breakfast in the morning, not realizing that for most of us, just having something to eat was a big deal. She stressed how important it was to have cereal for breakfast. The next day she asked how many of us had cereal that morning. We all raised our hands and she was very pleased. She then asked "Yoshito, Kazuo, Donald, what did you have?" When we all answered "rice," she admonished us, "Rice is not cereal!"

August Ahrens had a small store across the street named Shinsato Store. It had ice cream, ice cake, crack seed, and other goodies for the kids to buy after school. One day, we were walking home with Francisco Baracao who lived in Waikele. He had a nickel, a whole nickel, and bought an ice cream cone, eating it as we walked. We weren't envious, we just accepted the fact that he had a cone and we didn't. Just as we reached his house, he came to the end of the cone and found a piece of paper that said "FREE!" He had won a free ice cream cone! He told us to wait while he ran back to the store. When he returned, walking as fast as he could, the cone was melting and he kept wiping it with a finger and licking the dripping ice cream. Then he handed it to us and said, "Here, it's yours!" I shall never forget his kindness and thoughtfulness.

My oldest brother, Henry, caught the train to attend McKinley High School in Honolulu. My middle brother, Alfred, traveled by train to Farrington. When they built Waipahu High School, it included seventh grade through high school, as there was no intermediate school in the area. My brother Ernest and I walked on the railroad tracks one mile to and from school each day. Our school district was from Hālawa to Kaʻena Point. Before Waipahu High was built, there was no school between Farrington, Leilehua in Wahiawā, and Waialua. The "powers that be" decided that building country schools was a waste of money. If you sent them to school, they would not work the plantations.

Since the school was brand new, we got to vote for our school colors; we chose blue and gold, and a contest was held to write the Alma Mater. Our cousin, Lorraine Ching, won. Then we needed a mascot. There were all kinds of suggestions but finally the nickname "Marauders" won out. Why the Marauders? Well, the time was just before World War II and all the military aircraft had nicknames. There was one solitary aircraft which flew out of Hickam everyday around noon to patrol. It was a B-26 made by the Martin Aircraft Co., called the Martin Marauder. As it passed over the school, one of the students remarked, "Eh, the Marauder." He sent in his entry and it was chosen as the nickname for the school's athletic teams.

Waipahu was a great learning experience. We studied vocational agriculture which sometimes seemed to consist only of working in the cane fields once a week, but we did learn how to graft plants and to air layer them.

We all had a home project. One of the students had a cow at home, so that became his project... keeping track of how much milk the cow produced. Since we had chickens at home, they became my project. I kept track of how many eggs were laid, and how many each hen laid; the low producers went into the pot.

Waipahu was a plantation community and the school reflected that. There was only one *haole* in my class; most Caucasians went to Punahou. There were very few Chinese as they had come a generation before and had already left the plantation. We had names for all the different races. Japanese were called: Buddha Heads"; we Chinese were "Pakes," Hawaiians were referred to as "Kanakas," and Koreans were called "Yobos." Filipinos were "Bayaos," Portuguese were "Portagee," and we called Puerto Ricans "Borinki." We used these names without any racial aspersions, nothing negative at all... just a matter of identification

December 7, 1941 shook us, and Hoʻaeʻae, out of a peaceful, almost dreamy existence. Ernest and I had spent the weekend in Honolulu with our older brothers and sisters. On Saturday, December 6, we went to the football game between University of Hawaiʻi and Willamette University. My sister, Bea, was secretary to Pump Searle, Athletic Director at the University, and had gotten us tickets. We stayed at our Honolulu house, which oldest brother, Henry, had the foresight to build. It was conveniently located in Makiki, and all the brothers and sisters who were working or going to the UH stayed there.

On Sunday, December 7, 1941, brother Alfred drove us home to Hoʻaeʻae, before going to Pearl Harbor, where he worked for Hawaiian Dredging which was doing some work there. We had just returned to our peaceful country home when the attack came. At first, we didn't know what was happening. All we saw was lots of black smoke coming from the main part of Pearl Harbor. Then we saw planes zooming over our house with the red ball of Japan under their wings. One plane crashed in the cane field which had just been harvested. We watched as shrapnel from bombs or anti-aircraft shells rained on the tin roof of our kitchen. We realized we were under attack!

The attack waxed and waned. Papa and Mama worried about Alfred who was at work at Pearl Harbor. In the late afternoon, a flight of B-17s flew over, heading east to seek out the Japanese. We still didn't quite grasp what was going on as all we had was a crystal set radio with head phones. The next day, everything was quiet so we went to school where we found the entire campus ringed with barbed wire. We were told that there would be no school until further notice.

After December 7, 1941, the Hoʻaeʻae that we knew did not exist. The train stopped running and we had curfews and blackouts. In April of 1942, we moved to Honolulu, to the house in upper Makiki where my older brothers and sisters were living. We made the move in a hired pick-up truck with side panels. The driver, Mama and Papa, my younger sister, Ruth, myself, and all of our worldly belongings were crammed into the truck and we made it in one trip. Welcome to the Big City!

The house where we lived was almost at the end of Makiki Street and we were the only non-*haole* family in the neighborhood. The children I played with went to Punahou and ʻIolani. Billy Haxton and I became the best of friends, and on Saturdays we'd walk down to the Palace Theatre on Beretania Street to see a movie. Billy went to Punahou and we often went to the Punahou pool to swim. The Haxtons had a very large yard and I spent a lot of time there. Mrs. Haxton would yell out, "Lunch time, Billy. You, too, Donald."

Schools opened in May of 1942 and I went to Stevenson Intermediate, an English Standard School. To be accepted, non-*haoles* were required to take an English test, oral and written, to prove that their English was sufficient. Fortunately I passed the test. The school wasn't too far from home, about one-and-a-half miles, so I walked, usually with some of my new friends. Before long it was time to move on to high school.

I will never forget my initiation to Roosevelt. Here I was, a "Country Jack" from "Waipahuey" ...the smallest boy in the class. My home room was 103, and when I finally found it, the teacher took one look at me and pointed out the window: "Lincoln (Elementary) School is down there." The entire class roared with laughter. *Kua'āina* that I was, I didn't even know what she was alluding to.

At Waipahu, it was not cool to show off that you were smart. Students sat in the back of the room and rarely raised their hands. At Roosevelt, the students were smart and proud of it. If you wanted to sit in the back? Plenty of room. The front was crowded and when a question was asked, there would be a forest of upraised hands clamoring for attention.

My salvation came in the pineapple fields. The entire school went every Monday as our contribution to the war effort. We were paid by age; the older ones got more. I got thirteen cents per hour; others got fifteen or seventeen cents. I was at home in my own element and would outwork everybody, even the big football boys. I overheard the teachers talking about that, which made me work even harder.

World War II had a profound effect on our lives. We lugged our gas masks everywhere, even to lunch time school dances. Army Special Services took over our auditorium but we got to see Maurice Evans in "Hamlet." During the Battle of Midway, planes were taking off from Hickam Air Force Base to seek the enemy. As time went by, the War moved farther and farther west towards Japan. We saw Honolulu jam-packed with soldiers, sailors, and marines, and Pearl Harbor filled with ships. One day they were all gone and everything was quiet. Then the news: our forces were landing in the Marshalls, the Marianas, and Okinawa. During a football game in 1944, Ralph Cote pointed out a B-29 Bomber flying over Waikīkī. He said, "That's the plane that is going to end the war." Sure enough, within a year, the B-29 Enola Gay, dropped the bomb, "Fat Boy," on Hiroshima.

The three years at Roosevelt were some of the best years of my life, although they were spent completely during the war. Despite the many restrictions, we managed to have a great time, and perhaps because of them, we developed a special closeness that somehow made our class special. The friends I made, the education I received, all had a great impact on my future. Graduation meant that soon I would be drafted. Another total change in lifestyle was ahead, but I was looking forward to it.

After graduating from Roosevelt, I attended the University of Hawai'i for a semester before I was drafted. After the war, I returned to UH and graduated in 1951. In 1952 I married Loretta Wong, from the island of Lānai'i. We have six children: three girls, three boys, and ten grand children. My first job was with the U.S. Fish and Wildlife Service doing oceanic and fisheries research. Next came a stint with the Social Security Administration in Hawai'i, Samoa, Guam, and San Francisco. My last career assignment was Resident Post Officer for the US Consumer Product Safety Commission, a one-person office, responsible for Hawai'i, Samoa and Guam. A nice way to end forty-four years of government service.

Mama doing business with lei sellers at Aloha Tower.

Donald (Front row right) with siblings.

JANICE AMANTE HOBSON MONRO

Both my parents' ancestors were originally from England. My father, Zeke Sebaldus Hobson, didn't know much about his family, but he was born in Fayetteville, North Carolina. After his mother died when he was just six years old, his father moved the family to Andalusia, Alabama, where his father remarried and had seven more children. At the tender age of sixteen, Daddy ran away from home and joined the Navy.

My mother, Genevieve Hood, traced her family history all the way back to Robin Hood. After arriving in America, her great-grandparents spent some time in Boston, Massachusetts, before traveling south to North Carolina, then Georgia, and finally settling permanently in Pensacola, Florida.

Daddy's first assignment in the Navy was in Pensacola, where a friend introduced him to my mother and they fell in love. It was devastating when he was shipped off, but they kept in close touch with each other.

When Daddy was about twenty-one years of age, he was stationed at Pearl Harbor in Hawai'i where he was assigned to a submarine. As soon as he was settled, he sent for Genevieve. It was 1926 and she was nineteen, just starting college and studying to become a school teacher. She was also teaching in the swampy, back woods of Florida in a one room school house near Tallahassee, where two of her students were as old as she. When she got his letter, she dropped everything, packed her bags, took the train to California, and got on a ship to Hawai'i. They were married the day the ship arrived. Only then did she send a telegram to her father to tell him where she was.

Eleven months later I was born at Queen's Hospital in Honolulu, delivered by two Navy doctors. The first time my parents went out alone after I was a born, I was taken to the submarine where my babysitters were a bunch of sailors.

Mother was determined to get her teaching degree, so she enrolled at the University of Hawai'i. She hired a wonderful Japanese maid, who she called *Mamasan,* to take care of me. Then Mother took me to the Big Island of Hawai'i with her when she was sent to a teaching school in Kealakekua. I was just two years old at the time, and since the school would not let her keep me in the dorm with her and the other young teachers, she boarded me with a Hawaiian family. (The Weeks family in Kona) I was just beginning to talk, and when Mother came to visit, all I could speak was Hawaiian. I lived with the family for two years and they were very good to me. The Weeks had several children, including a daughter, Thelma, who was about six years old. She thought I had been *hānai* to the family, so she treated me as her new little sister. I was told she loved me very much, and I have always remembered her with pleasant thoughts. They say she cried for weeks when Mother took me back to Honolulu.

When we went to the Big Island, we traveled on cattle boats, and Mother got seasick as the ocean was very rough between the Islands. The awful smell of cattle didn't help either, but there were no planes yet. When Hawaiian Airlines started up in 1929, the planes were very small and Mother got motion sickness whenever she had to go back to the Big Island for special classes. When she returned, Daddy and I would go to the airport to pick her up and he would always bring a bucket, towel, and bowl of ice for her.

In 1931, I was blessed with a baby sister who was named Patricia Ann; we called her Patsy. When I was three and a half years old, we moved near the fire station at the end of Koko Head Avenue in Kaimukī. There were lots of kids to play with, and one day a little boy had a nickel and he asked me to go with him to buy an ice cream cone. The only place we knew to get one was about two miles away on Waiʻalae Avenue. So down the street we traipsed, me in just my little panties, both of us bare footed, and he with his five cents. We hadn't thought to ask our parents... we just started walking, looking forward to the ice cream. It must have taken us two hours to get there, and just as we were getting close to the ice cream shop, a car hit my little friend and knocked him down. Fortunately, he wasn't badly hurt. It had never occurred to us that we had done anything wrong, but when the police drove us home, and our parents found out where we had been, they were terribly upset. After all that, we didn't get any ice cream!

When I was about six years old, my parents built a large house on Sierra Drive. What a wonderful view we had! We could look right into Diamond Head Crater and see all the way to the ocean. We could even see Daddy's submarine and on the day we knew he'd be coming home, I would run down the street to a house that had a big plumeria tree, pick flowers, take them home, and string a lei for him. Then we'd drive to Pearl Harbor to greet him as his ship pulled into the dock.

Even at six years of age, I was allowed to catch two buses and ride to Waikīkī by myself to take hula lessons at Lalani Hawaiian Village on the corner of Paoakalani and Kalākaua Avenues. It was close to the zoo, so we often went there after class. Actually, it wasn't much of a zoo back then; just a huge tortoise, some monkeys in a cage, ducks in a duck pond, and an elephant, but we loved to go there!

I started school at Aliʻiōlani, where Mrs. Sterns was my first and second grade teacher. The girls at school put on a dance show every year. One year our costumes were very fancy, made of black and white satin, and we wore tap shoes. Another year we dressed like pirates, with bandanas on our heads and I carried a wooden sword. My favorite teacher, Mrs. Johnson, had a big Mexican sombrero and taught us to do the Mexican Hat Dance.

A favorite event at school was May Day. Every year there was a lei-making contest and once I made a lei of Primo beer caps (Daddy drank a lot of beer) and entered it in the contest. I won first prize for the most unusual lei. I remember it was very heavy! To make it, I had to take out the cork and punch a hole in the cap, then string each one on a piece of cord.

One day, Mother took Patsy and me to Waikīkī to the Uluniu Women's Swim Club. While we were there, we heard a big commotion on the beach and ran out to see what it was all about. It was Bing Crosby on his honeymoon, walking by with his wife, Dixie. We all ran up to him and asked for his autograph. The only problem was, I didn't have any paper for him to write on. When he realized that, he said, "If you can run fast and get some, I'll wait for you." I ran as fast as I could to my mother but all she had was the paper from a stick of chewing gum. I didn't think he'd really be waiting, but he was, and nicely signed my gum wrapper.

Shirley Temple was a frequent visitor to Honolulu, and when she arrived on a Matson steamship, Mother would take us down to the pier to greet her. Then we'd quickly drive to the Royal Hawaiian Hotel and watch her walk up the stairs to the entrance. There were always crowds of little girls there, thrilled to catch a glimpse of their idol.

I frequently complained about not having any relatives nearby like most of my friends, so in the middle of the sixth grade, my parents sent me to Florida to become acquainted with my maternal relatives. I stayed with my grandparents in Pensacola, and learned how to live like a mainland kid, walking to school in cold weather. All the children in my class thought I lived in a grass shack with no bathroom, but in Florida, most of them still had outhouses.

When I returned to Hawai'i, it was time to start the eighth grade. I entered Robert Louis Stevenson Intermediate School where I found many of my old friends and classmates from Ali'iolani, and made new friends as well. Dances were held upstairs on the second floor, although the building was in bad shape, almost to the point of being dangerous. But the music was great, it was recess, so we didn't really care.

The "in" thing for girls to wear in those days was a pleated, white sharkskin skirt with a sweater, saddle shoes and bobby socks. We must have been hot as there was no air-conditioning then, but I don't remember it ever bothering me. Being "in style" was far more important.

When the ninth grade started in September of 1941, we all felt so grown-up. We were thoroughly enjoying our last year at Stevenson, although we could hardly wait to get to Roosevelt High School. Mother drove Patsy and me to school, but coming home, we took the bus or street car to Koko Head Avenue. There was always a large group of us and we piled into a small bus to take us up Sierra Drive. That little bus really struggled to make it up the hill, but it always did, while we all sang "The Old Gray Mare, She Ain't What She Used to Be." When we got to my house, I hated to get off…the ride was so much fun.

In 1941 Dad had an opportunity to move us into brand new Naval Housing, then under construction at Pearl Harbor. While waiting, we sold our home on Sierra Drive, and rented a place temporarily on Koko Head Avenue. We planned to move in on December 7. Early that morning, while we were trying to awaken Daddy, a car drove up the hill with its horn blaring. We ran to the window and looked out to see Daddy's friend and fellow navy-man, Mr. Boggan, dragging his daughter, Joan, then six or seven years old, up the steps to our house, with Mrs. Boggan hurrying behind. We couldn't imagine what was wrong until Mr. Boggan started yelling, "The God-damn Japs are bombing the hell out of Pearl Harbor!" I quickly turned on the radio and they were playing a popular tune, "I Don't Want to Set the World on Fire." Then the announcer abruptly broke in and said, "Pearl Harbor is under attack, everybody take cover!"

Daddy quickly got up, dressed, and told me to run around the neighborhood to tell any of the servicemen who lived nearby that if they wanted a ride to the base, to come quickly and ride with him and Mr. Boggan. At house after house, they thought I was a kid pulling a joke, but as I kept running, I yelled at them to turn on their radio.

Mr. Boggan was already living at Naval Housing, and he told us that the Japanese planes were flying very low, right down their street, to bomb the ships. Mrs. Boggan and Joan stayed with us, and another Navy friend brought his wife and baby daughter to our house before he hurried back to the base.

After I called on all the military houses, I ran over to Center Street to a home on the side of the hill that had big mango trees where I could see the bombing going on at Pearl Harbor and Hickam Field. Other people came along, and soon there was a large group of us watching the awful destruction. We were all upset and didn't know what to do. Finally, I went home and found that everyone had decided to go up to the top of Wilhelmina Rise to a friend's big home where we felt we'd be safe, especially since there was a man there. But just as we started up the hill, we saw planes flying toward us, so mother quickly turned the car around and drove back to our garage. Everyone jumped out and ran into the house... just in time! I looked out the window and saw the Japanese bombers with the emblem of the rising sun beneath their wings. They were so low I could even see the heads of the pilots.

Later on, when things had quieted down, we got in the car again and Mother drove us up the hill to our friend's home. From there, we could see Pearl Harbor and Hickam Field burning, as well as other places around the city... the flames were shooting high in the sky. The next day we drove back to our house and the two other mothers and children stayed with us for nearly two weeks. Fortunately, Mother had gone to the commissary the day before, and had bought a lot of extra groceries.

It was over a week before we heard from Daddy and Mr. Boggan. Then one day Mr. Boggan appeared and told us that they were all safe. He talked briefly to Mrs. Boggan and Joan before heading back to work. He wanted to see his family because he was assigned to a very dangerous mission; he was being sent to Bellows Air Field to remove a live bomb from a Japanese submarine that the two-man crew had abandoned when they jumped out; one man drowned and the other was captured by a big Hawaiian from Waimānalo. Mr. Boggan brought many things out of the sub that were sent to President Roosevelt but was allowed to keep several of the items. Some he gave to Mother to take to her school to show the children.

About a week after the bombing, our dear old *Mamasan* came by one day, and tearfully told Mother how very sorry she was. Mother told her we didn't blame her at all, and not to ever think we would; we still loved her as much as ever.

Schools remained closed for three months; we were issued special IDs and gas masks which we had to have with us at all times, even when we slept; to be sure our masks worked, we had to go through a tent of gas. We spent our time tearing and folding sheets for bandages for the Red Cross, and did whatever we were asked to do.

Around February, Mother, Patsy, and I were given the opportunity to go to the mainland, which Mother and Daddy decided was a good idea. It took us eight, very cold and miserable days to reach San Francisco, as we were part of a convoy that zigged and zagged over the ocean. Our ship was the former Matson Navigation Company's luxury liner, Lurline, which had been stripped of its elegance and turned into a troop ship.

When I started school in the tenth grade at Pensacola High, I was happy to find some old friends from the year I spent with my grandparents. It was the same school mother and her siblings had attended, and some of her teachers were still there. We stayed for a year, and Patsy and I often went with Mother to military camps to help entertain the troops with shows arranged by the Red Cross. We did the hula in our grass skirts and sometimes traveled for hours on a weekend to do a show.

One day Mother heard that there was a serious shortage of school teachers in Hawai'i. She applied and was accepted in June of 1943. The train ride back to California was terrible! It was so crowded we had to stand all the way and sleep on the floor at night; it took three days to get there. Then we had to wait a few days before boarding a huge transport ship that was shipping troops to the war zones. We were part of a convoy again and it took us eight days to reach Hawai'i. When we finally arrived, Daddy was there to greet us and it was a wonderful, albeit teary, reunion. As we didn't have a house yet, we stayed with friends at Naval Housing until my parents found a house for sale within easy walking distance of Stevenson Intermediate and Roosevelt High Schools, where Patsy and I would be going.

I loved Roosevelt and it was great seeing lots of old friends, although there were many war restrictions in place. Once a week we went to work doing manual labor in the pineapple fields in Wahiawā. When I developed a bad case of hay fever, I was sent to work in the Dole Pineapple Cannery instead.

My boy friend, Tim Monroe, quit school in his senior year to join the Navy and was stationed at Pearl Harbor. A few months later, he was sent to boot camp on the mainland where he was not allowed to communicate with anyone. After not hearing from him for six weeks, I thought we were through.

Just one week before the A Bomb was dropped; I met a young service man that I began to date. In a very short time he asked me to marry him and I accepted. My parents liked him, but of course I had to finish high school first. It was a sad day when I learned that I would not be able to graduate with my class as my school records for the year I had spent in Pensacola did not arrive in time. Instead of marching up the aisle to get my diploma, I served as an usherette, seating the friends and relatives who came to see their dear ones graduate.

Forced to repeat my senior year, it was not a happy time for me as my fiancée, Clayton, went back to his home in San Antonio not long after the war ended. I managed to get through the year, but my thoughts were more on my wedding than on graduation. In fact, I graduated in my wedding dress.

After high school, I moved to San Antonio, Texas where I married Clayton Wall. We had three daughters and four grandchildren. I was a Brownie and Girl Scout leader when my girls were in school, and my hobby was landscaping, not only my yard, but my neighbors as well. After living in San Antonio for almost 49 years, my husband died suddenly in March of 1995. I decided to take a trip back to Hawai'i to attend my 50th class reunion and it was there that I was re-acquainted with my high school boyfriend, Tim Monroe. We were married in 1996 and moved to Waimea-Kamuela on the Big Island. Tim passed away in 2005 and I returned to the mainland. I now live in a retirement community in Portland, Oregon.

Janice in hula attire

Patsy, Mom and Janice

Zeke and Genevieve Hobson

CHARLES AMOR

My father, Simeon Amor, was born in 1894 in Dumangete, Negros Oriental, Philippines, an archipelago consisting of over 7,200 separate islands; Negros Oriental is among the southern islands called the Visayas. After completing high school, he made his way to Manila, and then on to Hawai'i to make a better life for himself.

Filipinos were recruited to work in the sugar fields in Hawai'i after the Chinese, Japanese, and Koreans who had preceded them. Families were not encouraged. Daddy (we pronounced it Dah day) and his friend, Modesto Salve, feigned lack of schooling and came to Hawai'i as plantation laborers. After Daddy's contract expired, he enlisted in the U.S. Army and was assigned to Schofield Barracks as a cook. He obtained his U.S. citizenship as a reward for being honorably discharged. In his middle years, he joined the American Legion. He was proud of his service to his adopted country.

My father was among a dozen Filipino males who were trained as ministers at Aldersgate Methodist Church on Liliha Street in Honolulu. Daddy was not ordained, but since he could speak English, as well as Spanish, and several Filipino dialects, his assignment was to relieve Filipino ministers who were ill or on sabbatical. Thus he served on all the major islands, and in return, received free lodging, gifts of food, and sometimes cash from parishioners.

My mother, Victoria Morillo was born in 1905, in Cebu City, Philippines, also in the southern islands. Like my father, she had a Spanish surname and spoke the Visayan dialect. The Spanish dominated the Philippines for hundreds of years and required Filipinos to adopt Spanish surnames.

Unlike most Filipinos, Mama came to Hawai'i with her family. Her father was a labor contractor whose mission was to escort the laborers on the ship and deliver them to the sugar plantations. When her father completed his contract, she refused to return to the Philippines with her family; she was left at the Susannah Wesley Home for Girls in Kalihi. The girls attended Kalihi Methodist Church, which is where Mama and Daddy met.

I was born at Queen's Hospital on January 13, 1928, the Chinese Year of the Dragon, the third of seven children; another child died in infancy. The first born was a boy, Simeon, followed by Esther, myself, then Mabel, Samuel, Winona and Paul. Because of Daddy's itinerant assignments, each of us was born on a different island.

During my pre-school years, Daddy's assignment was at a sugar plantation in Pāhala, on the island of Hawai'i. I was placed in the care of my Godparents who lived at the Filipino camp located near the plantation. Each ethnic group had a separate camp, and the plantation provided free housing and medical services. Food, and all other goods, were purchased at the company store. The family lived a frugal life, and to save money, my Godparents raised vegetables and kept a few pigs for sale or barter. They also kept fighting chickens for recreation and gambling.

The Filipino camp was serviced by a dusty, unpaved dirt road. As the camp was just a few hundred yards below the sugar mill, it was noisy throughout the harvesting season. Grinding often went on for twenty four hours at a time.

The Filipino Camp adjoined the Japanese Camp. In the center was a community bathhouse featuring a large Japanese *furo,* or bathtub, made of wood. The bathtub was deep, and after a hard days' work in the cane fields, a hot soak was a treat. The Filipinos shared the bathhouse with the Japanese; first come, first served. The bathhouse was divided by a partition to separate the males from the females.

When my family moved to Hilo at the end of Daddy's assignment, I joined them there. In contrast, Hilo seemed so green! It drizzled every day and there were frequent heavy rains. The roofs of houses were made of corrugated iron and the sound of rain splattering on the roofs was almost melodious. The sound would lull me to sleep.

I entered Kapi'olani School at age five, which accounts for my graduation from high school at seventeen. We lived in Villa Franca, a working class neighborhood, which was later destroyed by the 1946 tsunami. Everyone walked to school shoeless; I didn't own a pair of shoes until I came to Honolulu many years later. After I completed the sixth grade, we moved to Haili Street, in the center of Hilo town. There were three churches, a Y.W.C.A., two basketball gyms, and the Lyman Museum... all within two blocks of our house. Each of the three churches had a bell which clanged noisily every Sunday. Also from our house we could hear the gong from the Buddhist temple six blocks away.

Our family drifted away from the Filipino Methodist Church as Daddy was only a lay minister and better trained ministers were available. I recall fighting in the church yard with the new Filipino minister's son. To this day I cannot recall the reason for the fight, but Haili Church became my sanctuary.

We lived in an elevated wooden house with the usual corrugated tin roof; it was located across from Haili Congregational Church, which we then attended. The church catered to Hawaiians, and its songs and sermons were a mix of Hawaiian and English. I joined the Boy's Choir which was conducted by Kihei Brown, a member of the Desha-Beamer extended family of musicians, who sang a beautiful falsetto. Kihei Brown did not think it unusual for a Filipino boy to sing in a Hawaiian choir.

Daddy had been unemployed for some time, although I wasn't aware of it. To learn a trade, he took a correspondence course in sign painting. One Monday morning when I was in the sixth grade, I went to the veranda where he was painting. I was dressed for school and asked him for my lunch money. He didn't look at me or say anything... he just kept painting. After my third request without a reply, I decided that I would have to find a way to earn money.

At Hilo Intermediate School, I met a Portuguese boy who took me to the printing press of the Hilo Tribune Herald. He showed me how to buy the afternoon papers, two for a nickel, and to sell them for a nickel apiece. By circling the small town twice before sundown, I was able to sell six papers a day... enough for my lunch money, with some left over. Saturday night was special because we sold the Sunday edition for ten cents each. We stood at the doors of the movie theater on Saturday night and as people left after the movie, I sold at least ten newspapers.

The beaches in Hilo were not fit for swimming so we went crabbing instead. On special Sundays, the family picnicked at Coconut Island. As a boy, the island looked very far away, but actually it is fewer than a hundred yards off-shore and a walkway has since been built to connect it with the mainland. My parents paid a boatman five cents to row us to the island and back.

Mama liked to gather *'opihi,* and the Hilo breakwater on the seaward side was covered with these delicious Hawaiian limpets. *'Opihi* was a prized delicacy that flourished on boulders constantly pounded by waves. The memory of Mama dodging the waves makes me cringe. Mabel, my younger sister, and I helped gather the *'opihi,* although I didn't acquire a taste for them until much later. (Today, a good *lu'au* is judged by the presence of *'opihi* on the menu.)

Daddy's sign painting business grew with the town. He was often contracted to make signs for retail stores and I went along, helping him carry his paints and brushes. Election campaign time was profitable for the family. Daddy was hired to make campaign signs because he was an artist as well as a painter, and his work was much in demand. The whole family was enlisted to help, and as a reward, we were taken to Mo'oheau Park to hear campaign speeches and meet the candidates.

I entered Hilo Intermediate School in the sixth grade and for the next three years, band was the class I most enjoyed. We got to take home the school instrument, which I did daily, even if I didn't practice. Our instructor was Mary Lou Drake, who had come from Texas, and this was her first teaching assignment. She was about five feet three inches tall, blond, and blue eyed; the first *haole* female I had ever seen up close. Of course, I had a crush on her. I sat in the first chair and played solo clarinet parts. In the sixth grade, the band marched in Hilo's Fourth of July Parade. Miss Drake, who was a baton twirler in college, taught me how to be the drum major for this event.

We kept a garden in the back yard where we grew sweet potatoes, tomatoes, eggplants, beans and Chinese cabbage. Mango and banana trees grew wild on the property. Just beyond our garden was an empty lot filled with guava trees which bore sweet, white guavas. After school I raced home to check on the trees, hoping to get the fruit before my sister, Mabel.

When my older brother, Sonny, graduated from Hilo High School, Dad took him and my older sister, Esther, to Honolulu where jobs were abundant because of the growing defense industry. Dad and Sonny were employed at Wheeler Field; Esther enrolled part-time at Farrington High School, and worked at Ford Island as an apprentice aircraft mechanic after school.

Since I was the oldest child at home, Dad wrote, addressing me "Master Charles Amor" and asked me to act as head of the family. Can you imagine how important I felt! I was in the ninth grade at Hilo Intermediate School, selling papers for spending money. When the Haili Church janitor left for a defense industry job, I was paid to sweep the church and mow the lawn. It helped to keep the family stable.

On Sunday morning, December 7, 1941, I was playing marbles under the *kamani* tree at Haili Church. It was not until later in the afternoon, when I turned on the radio to listen to "Your Hit Parade," that I learned about the Pearl Harbor attack. I remember the radio announcer saying that tap water was not safe to drink because of the possibility of infiltrators poisoning the water supply. The warning was ignored. The next day, Mama sent me to the Hilo Macaroni Factory to buy a large container of saloon pilot crackers. This was our reserve should food became scarce. We were instructed to blacken all the windows and remain indoors after sundown. Block Wardens were appointed to strictly enforce the curfew and blackout. About a week later, Kilauea volcano erupted. The light was so bright at night that you could read a newspaper outdoors. So much for blackouts!

After the December 7th attack, Daddy was reassigned from Bellows Field to Hickam Field. This made him eligible for civilian housing. Not long after, Dad sent for us, and Mom and we four children moved to Honolulu.

Honolulu was very different from Hilo; it was warmer and more humid. I felt sticky and uncomfortable the first few weeks. To a Hilo boy, Honolulu was a real city. I was entranced by the electric trolleys on King Street. The ride on leather seats was quiet and smooth. Aloha Tower was the tallest building I had seen in my life. The Chinatown markets, with numerous vendors' stalls, were crowded with people purchasing fresh fish, meat, and vegetables. Further along Hotel Street was a sea of uniforms. Servicemen were present everywhere: sailors, soldiers, marines, all seeking some type of amusement.

Hickam housing, where we lived, was designed for civilian employees working at Hickam Air Base. At the rear of each duplex were ground level dirt mounds hollowed inside to be used as air raid shelters. Directly in front of our house was a water tank where the trains restocked their water supply. The area was once called, "Watertown."

When Mama went to work as a janitress at Pearl Harbor Naval Shipyard, we children had to fend for ourselves. I asked a young neighbor boy what school he attended. "Be at this bus stop tomorrow morning at 8:00 a.m. sharp, and a free military bus will take you there," he replied. Later I learned that his name was Stanley Alama and the school was Robert Louis Stevenson, then located at Kapālama. Stevenson was a feeder school to Roosevelt High School, which was then an English Standard School where a reading test was required for admittance. Luckily, I passed. My other siblings wound up at Kalākaua Intermediate School. I've always been grateful to Stanley for taking me to Stevenson. The Stevenson campus was taken over by the military after December 7 and turned into a hospital, so Kapālama School shared its facilities; we had sessions at Kapālama in the morning and at Stevenson in the afternoon.

I soon made lots of friends and on Saturdays we usually attended the matinee at Hawaii Theater. Otherwise, we took the HRT (Honolulu Rapid Transit) bus to the Natatorium. It was a huge salt water swimming pool located just beyond Waikīkī. It was famous for its high diving board. Sometimes we took the bus to the end of the line to what is now Hawaii Kai. Then we hiked up the hill to Hanauma Bay.

I was new to Honolulu and everything was an adventure. Ralph Cote introduced me to the Navy Recreation Center just outside the Pearl Harbor gates. The Center had a new bowling alley, but no pin-setting machines, so I got a job setting pins. A good pinsetter could manage two alleys at once and double the tips. As soon as I got home, Mother emptied my pockets and gave me an allowance. Whenever I needed money, I set pins.

After Stevenson I went to Roosevelt High School. There I hung out with friends on the patio or under the huge Chinese banyan tree. Students of different ethnic groups had their own territory and seemed to know where they belonged. To me, the most outstanding thing about Roosevelt was the presence of so many gorgeous girls, especially upper classmen. The *haole* girls on the military bus were pretty, but the local girls at Roosevelt were exotic; they were of every ethnic mixture and carried themselves gracefully compared to Hilo girls. Comparing the different ethnic combinations, I favored the mixture of Hawaiian and Chinese, but I was too shy to approach any females. "Besides", I asked myself, "what gorgeous *hapa-haole* girl would be interested in a short Filipino boy like me?" The girls remained on a pedestal throughout high school.

Student assemblies featured talented and gorgeous cheer leaders. Their singing captured my heart. I thought how lucky I was to be at this school. Band was still my favorite class, especially since Miss Mary Lou Drake from Hilo was the instructor. Again I sat in the first chair in Band classes.

The military and defense industry had siphoned off the manpower from the plantations, so all high school students were required to work in the pineapple fields one day a week; for Roosevelt, it was Monday. The pineapple trucks picked up the students at the campus. Those of us from military housing stood at the edge the highway and were picked up on the way to Wahiawā.

I remember two types of assignments: picking slips for planting, and harvesting pineapples. The slips had been previously counted so when your assigned rows were finished, your job was done. This was called, *huki pau.* We wore canvas aprons to harvest the pineapple. We picked the ripened ones, placed them in our aprons. Then we walked to the beginning of the row and put the pineapples into crates. The loss of one school day each week appeared to have a major negative impact on my learning; I just wasn't prepared for higher education.

Some friends and I joined the Hawaii Defense Volunteers, a quasi-military unit, whose mission was to augment the activated Hawaii National Guard. We were issued uniforms and shotguns and assigned to guard sensitive targets like the water supply or electrical stations. We were taught to fire 30 caliber rifles, 12 gauge shotguns, and 45 caliber pistols. On a spring break, Ben Kittle and Ralph Cote persuaded some of us in the HDV to hike to the ridge of the Ko'olau summit and camp out there for three days. Eight of us in our HDV uniforms, on an unsanctioned activity, loaded with supplies to last us three days, negotiated the Makalapa Bridge, hiked to the foot of Hālawa Quarry, and entered the long winding trail to the summit, a distance that seemed like twenty miles due to its winding nature. The uphill climb, with our packs weighing at least fifty pounds, was arduous. Halfway up we were caught in a torrential rain storm, but we slogged onward to make the summit before sundown. Our reward on reaching the top was a magnificent view of Kāne'ohe Bay. The return hike was not as bad because the terrain looked familiar and we were going down hill. It was quite an achievement to have completed the hike without an accident.

That first summer, Vernon McMillan and Ralph Cote found me a job at the Navy Personnel Office Building, working in a small coffee shop. The next summer, after reaching age sixteen, I got a job at Pearl Harbor Navy Supply as a store clerk. Mr. Henry Kealoha, a happy Hawaiian, was my boss. His passion was volley ball, so exactly at noon every day, he set up a volleyball court outside the shop, and this became the gathering place for athletes.

My high school years flew by. There was always so much to do that class work took a back seat. Somehow school work didn't seem important, so I took the minimum number of classes to graduate. I spent graduation day at Waikiki Beach, sadly contemplating my foolishness for not taking advantage of the academic opportunities offered at Roosevelt. I knew before long I would be joining the Military, but since I was just seventeen, it was a year away. I sat on the sand and reminisced about the wonderful friends and the great adventures I had at Roosevelt, and even though I was not an outstanding student, I was grateful for the opportunity to attend that special school.

My next journey in life was sailing to California where I attended Fresno State College. I graduated in 1949 with a degree in Philosophy-Psychology. During the Korean conflict, I was drafted into the army and assigned to Tripler Army Hospital in Honolulu. After the war, I was employed as an Adult Probation Officer for the First Circuit Court, then appointed as the first State Director of the Commission on Aging. I left that position to become the Kalihi-Pālama Representative of the Concentrated Employment Program, a federal effort to recruit, train, and create employment for disadvantaged people. In 1968, I started the Hawai'i State Senior Center at Lanakila under the sponsorship of the University of Hawaii and assisted in the National Standards for Senior Centers for the Federal Government. I married Tatsue Yamamoto of Apia, Maui, who served as a State Parole Officer. We met as we both started our careers in social work. We have two sons. Tatsue passed away in 1995. As a retiree, I participate in daily exercise and educational programs such as social dancing, Tai Chi, men's hula, and 'ukulele.

The Amor Family, Charles on left.   *Charles and classmate Vernon McMillan*

LORRAINE "BROWNIE" BROWN WILLIAMS

My roots go back to the Island of Hawai'i where my maternal relatives lived in the heart of Waimea. My great-grandmother, Kapahu, was pure Hawaiian and my great-grandfather, Chong Ki, was pure Chinese. They had five children, one of whom was my grandmother. It was in Waimea that my grandparents met and married; my mother Mary, and her sister were both born there.

Mother moved to Honolulu to attend Normal School, which later became Stevenson Intermediate. Not long after graduation, she married and remained on O'ahu. Thus my brother Charles and I are a mixture of Hawaiian, Chinese, and *haole,* the latter from our father who was a mixture of Hawaiian and *haole*. I was born on August 23, 1926; my brother is three years older than I.

My maternal grandmother watched us while our parents were at work and a cousin lived with us after his mother died in childbirth. After living in Kaimukī for a few years, we moved to the McCully area where our house was close to the streetcar line. We once had a litter of puppies that sometimes wandered onto the tracks. When they did, the driver would stop the streetcar, clang the bell, and we would rush out to rescue our babies. When I was ten years old, we moved to Waikīkī and remained there throughout my teenage years.

The first school I attended was Sacred Hearts Convent which was located adjacent to the Cathedral of Our Lady of Peace on Fort Street, in the heart of downtown Honolulu. It was an imposing two-story structure, built in a square with a courtyard in the center filled with giant tamarind trees where we played during recess. The property went from Fort to Bishop Street, and extended from the Cathedral to S. H. Kress, our popular five and dime store. The school was surrounded by a wall, and every morning we entered through two enormous wooden doors. There was a large sitting room and the office of Reverend Mother, the principal; there were classrooms on both sides, as well as the second floor. The Belgian nuns spoke French, and although they were strict, they were also very kind. Our uniforms were a heavy, white cotton middy blouse with a black serge collar trimmed with white stripes and matching cuffs. The skirt, held up by suspenders, was black, pleated serge.

In 1938 the school moved to a larger area in Nu'uanu next to Nu'uanu stream. Our priest, Father Justin, had to cross the stream to get to the school and chapel as his small home was on other side. After school, we often lingered along Nuʻuanu Avenue near the wall to wave at the boys from ʻIolani School when they walked by.

After moving to Waikīkī, I attended St. Augustine's School on ʻŌhua Avenue, just a block from our house. The nuns, who belonged to the Maryknoll order which was headquartered in up-state New York, were far less strict than those at the convent, yet I missed the French accents and more elaborate habits of the other sisters.

In those days, except for the Moana and Royal Hawaiian Hotels, as well as a few small inns, Waikīkī was a residential neighborhood and a wonderful place to grow up. Grand mansions lined the waterfront, but the area *mauka* of Kalākaua Avenue was a neighborhood of charming little cottages with neatly manicured lawns and picket fences. On Kalākaua, there were grocery stores like Piggly Wiggly and Central Market, Blackshear's Drug Store, curio shops and restaurants. There was a bar called The Trump that was a popular gathering place. Our home was on Liliʻuokalani Avenue, *mauka* of Kūhiō, not far from ʻĀinahau, the former Cleghorn estate and home of Princess Kaʻiulani.

We were free to wander around the neighborhood as it was safe and friendly. My best friend was Ginny Shipley, who lived next door, and we loved to roam the area. Ginny was so agile that she could traipse along the horizontal two-by-fours that were part of the fences, and I finally acquired the art of balancing on them too. We often hopped down to pick up ripe dates that fell from the many date palms along the way. What a delicious snack!

My maternal grandmother, Koki, often took us to visit family on the north shore of Oʻahu, near the site of the present Turtle Bay Resort. We took the street car from Waikīkī to Dillingham Depot in Iwilei. From there we boarded the train which went along the Waiʻanae Coast, around Kaʻena Point, through Mokulēʻia, Haleʻiwa, Sunset Beach, and Kawela Bay. The house was located on a high, sandy hill from which there was a magnificent view of the enormous waves we loved to watch, but never dared to enter.

Another special memory is traveling by train to visit my paternal grandmother Brown, who lived on a homestead beachfront property in Nānākuli. She lived in a little wooden house with an outhouse. The shoreline in front of her home was rocky, and when we were there, we usually spent our time swimming and playing in the water.

When I was around ten years old, I learned to surf at Waikīkī and went with my friends to "Baby Surf," noted for its small waves. Just beyond was Queen's Surf, where the waves were much larger. Nearby was Waikīkī Tavern, a large two-story English Tudor-style building which housed a small hotel and shops, as well as a restaurant and bar. It was located on the beach near the Diamond Head end of Kalākaua, near Judge Steiner's home; it was a favorite place for breakfast with our families and friends.

Fort DeRussy was our usual destination for swimming, although we made a lot of stops along the way, including the majestic Royal Hawaiian Hotel where we loved to roam. We soon discovered the staircase that led to the tower, which, next to Aloha Tower, was probably the tallest structure in Honolulu at the time. No one ever questioned us when we made our way up to the top and surveyed the panoramic view. With no high rises to block them out, we could see the mountains and valleys stretched along the Koʻolau Range. Magnificent rainbows frequently arched across Mānoa or Pālolo, and we could see the full length of the Ala Wai Canal which stretched from the Diamond Head end of Waikīkī out to the ocean at Ala Moana. Sometimes we roller skated along the pathways that wandered through the hotel's lush, tropical gardens. Along the paths were canvas swings.

We often saw famous movie stars such as Bing Crosby, Loretta Young, Rochelle Hudson, and Nelson Eddy sitting under umbrellas on the beach in front of the hotel, as well as child stars Bobby Breen and Shirley Temple. They were always friendly, and happy to give us their autographs.

After leaving the Royal, we strolled along the shore until we came to Gray's Beach and the Halekulani Hotel, which had a stone wall across its beach-front. In the ocean below, huge beds of *limu* rose from the coral on the ocean floor, and when it reached the surface, swayed in and out with the tide. We always went down to the beach to pick some crispy stems to eat right then and there, and usually took more home for a snack to eat later with poi.

Fort DeRussy's major attractions were a large raft that floated off shore and a platform with a diving board set right in the water. We spent hours jumping off the raft and swimming around it.

Besides going to the beach, there were many other fun things to do in Waikīkī. A miniature golf course on Kalākaua Avenue was a place to celebrate birthdays and special occasions; the zoo was just a few short blocks away. We all loved Daisy the elephant, although it was sad to see her chained to a metal ring anchored in the cement. There was also a polar bear in a lava rock structure kept cool with huge blocks of ice. Then there was a fenced-in area with a kangaroo and an ostrich. We rode our bikes around the neighborhood, but never ventured beyond the Royal in one direction, or Kapiʻolani Park in the other.

We sometimes walked to the Kapahulu Theater in the afternoon to see a movie, but on Saturday morning, we took the bus downtown to the Princess Theater on Fort Street for the Mickey Mouse Club. Before the movies started, there was organ music played by Edwin Sawtelle, sing-a-longs with the audience and an Amateur Hour where young people performed... some dancing, some singing, others playing the accordion. We always stopped at the Chinese store located right next door to buy *manapua, pepeiao,* rice cake, crack seed and *see moi* to eat while enjoying the movie. After eating the meat off the seeds, we licked the bag for the last remaining bit of delicious sauce.

Another wonderful memory is walking along the beach in the evening and passing the Banyan Tree Court at the Moana Hotel. Two young Beamer cousins, Mahi and Keola, who were about ten years old, danced the hula there one night a week, accompanied by Keola's parents on the guitar and ʻukulele. It was great entertainment and the tourists loved it!

Because Mother worked, grandmother did all the cooking. She often made large pots of stew, and poi was served with every meal. A favorite dinner was white crab which friends often gave us. Grandma would boil them and lay them on newspapers on the table. We eagerly broke open the shells, removed the meat with our fingers, and devoured the luscious treat. The best part was there were no dishes to wash. We simply rolled up the newspapers and threw them away.

Ginny and I often wandered down to play in Princess Kaʻiulani's famous banyan tree on Tusitala Street. Ginny climbed up to the higher branches, but I stayed on the lower limbs close to the trunk except for one day when I ventured up to a very high branch. I was so frightened I never went near the tree again!

One of the little inns in Waikīkī was located on Koa Avenue and every summer when the circus came to town, the midgets that performed in a side show stayed there. All the neighborhood kids wandered down on their bikes to see them. They were always friendly, and seemed to look forward to our visits. We learned not to see them as freaks, but as real human beings.

Most of us learned to swim in deep water at the Natatorium, a 100-meter-long salt water pool completed in 1927 to honor those from Hawai'i who lost their lives in World War I. We taught ourselves deep water swimming by hanging on to the sides of the pool. There was a very high diving board, but I never had the nerve to climb up there, although I imagine the view was wonderful. Across the street was Kapi'olani Park with its band stand where the Royal Hawaiian Band gave a concert every Sunday afternoon

On the far Diamond Head side of the park, across Pākī Avenue, was a riding stable named Town and Country Stables, and next to it was the O'ahu Polo and Racing Club. In the park itself was a polo field where you could watch the matches for free just by driving your car up to the fence that surrounded it, or sitting on the grass to enjoy the game. There was lots of excitement when O'ahu's biggest rival, the Maui team, came to town. During the war, General Patton played on the Army team.

One of our favorite eating places in Waikīkī was Unique Lunch Room located on Kalākaua Ave across from the wall, which is now Kūhiō Beach. Our favorite order was *pipikaula* and *poi,* which cost the grand sum of fifteen cents, followed by a slice of delicious custard pie.

On the corner of Kalākaua and Lili'uokalani was the Giant Malt Shop owned by Mr. Mitchell. It was very popular with all the neighbors and beachgoers. Their malts, which cost fifteen cents, were so huge it took at least two people to finish one, and the assortment of flavors was enormous. Grape was my favorite.

We lived a wonderful, carefree lifestyle in Waikīkī, which was almost like a small island, bordered by the Ala Wai Canal on one side, and the ocean on the other. Then everything changed. One Saturday I spent the night with my friend, Loretta Carter, who lived *mauka* of Kalākaua Avenue across from Fort DeRussey. We were awakened early the next morning by the sound of heavy artillery which we assumed, like so many others, was simply anti-aircraft practice at Pearl Harbor. It was a common occurrence, one that we were used to hearing, and thought nothing of. Suddenly the phone rang; it was my mother calling to tell us that the Japanese were bombing Pearl Harbor. We were all shocked with the news and Loretta's parents at first refused to believe it until they turned on the radio. The announcer repeated over and over, "The island of O'ahu is under attack! Everybody take cover! The island of O'ahu is under attack! Everybody take cover!"

On that unforgettable day, the attack was so sudden we barely knew what was happening. Life changed in so many ways... all the things we were used to were suddenly not there any more.

No cars were allowed on the streets, so I stayed at Loretta's for several days. Schools closed, buses stopped running, gasoline, food and liquor were rationed, and martial law went in effect. Our dollar bills were stamped with the word H A W A I I, in case we were taken over by enemy forces. The island was surrounded with barbed wire, preventing access to the beaches, including Waikīkī. We were issued gas masks which we had to carry with us at all times. It was truly a frightening experience.

Suddenly the Island was crowded with men from all branches of the service, and Waikīkī was a popular place for them to visit. Not long after, the luxurious Royal Hawaiian Hotel was taken over by the Navy as a place for R&R (Rest and Recreation) for submariners.

When school resumed after a three month hiatus, I decided to go to Roosevelt with many of my friends. Even the school was surrounded by barbed wire as the Navy had taken over the athletic field and the gym. We even had some sailors in our classes.

From the first day, I liked the school; I found many old friends, and made new ones. I spent most of recess time on the patio, a popular hangout in front of the main building. Occasionally we went down to the lawn to sit under the huge Chinese banyan tree in front of the school to play a card game called *kāmau*, a simple form of bridge.

On Mondays, we went to work in the pineapple fields. Crowded onto the back of a truck with long benches, wearing long pants, long sleeved shirts, and wide brimmed straw hats, we sang all the way out to Wahiawā. Once in the fields, we sweltered in the heat and dust, twisting fruit off the stems and putting them into gunny sacks. We brought our own lunch which we ate outdoors. There was a *luna* who passed out goggles when we arrived and kept an eagle-eye on us at all times to make sure we put in our day's work.

Some of the braver, more *kolohe* kids, snuck off to the irrigation ditch to smoke cigarettes or just goof off, something I never dreamed of trying. We were paid seventeen-and-a-half cents an hour.

The rest of the week we were in class from 8:00 a.m. until 3:00 p.m. My favorite class was Home Economics where our teacher, Mrs. Paulus, taught us to cook delicious meals. Spanish rice was my favorite and I still make it to this day.

Eventually, intramural sports resumed and football games were our biggest events. We had really good teams in '44 and '45 when 'Iolani, an all-boys school, closed for the duration; most of the players on their championship team came to Roosevelt. Our big rival was Punahou and our students would sneak over at night and paint their dome Roosevelt colors, red and yellow. And of course, Punahou students retaliated by painting our dome yellow and blue. But it was an affable rivalry with many friendships between students of both schools.

After school we often rode the bus downtown to Hollister's Drug Store for a yummy hot fudge sundae. We also hung out at Benson Smith drug store and spent time at their soda fountain, along with kids from other schools. (We were always checking out the cute guys from Kamehameha.) Liberty House was Honolulu's only big department store, and at Christmas time we loved to visit the store just to see its magnificent Christmas tree.

In 1942, sponsored by Charlie Amalu and Willie Whittle, I joined the Outrigger Canoe Club where I already knew a lot of people. The ones I didn't know, I soon made friends with. When paddling season started, I was lucky enough to paddle as one of Johnny Hollinger's crew, along with Lois Gilman, Blondie Boyd, and my close friend, Loretta Carter. Johnny also taught me how to steer a two-man canoe, and I often invited someone to join me and ride the waves at Canoes Surf.

When I wasn't in the water, I was on the volleyball court, usually the "baby court," or at the snack bar having the most popular item on the menu, a bowl of stew, gravy and rice which cost fifteen cents.

One of my most vivid memories of the Outrigger, and certainly the most unpleasant, was a day, during the war, when I was standing in the lobby talking with a group of people. Someone threw a canister of tear gas right in front of us and instantly our eyes and skin began to burn. We all dashed into the locker rooms, heading for the showers. When that didn't ease the smarting, someone shouted, "Head for the ocean!" and we made a dash to the beach and jumped into the water. It was quite a while before the pain went away.

Meanwhile, our school days at Roosevelt were passing by too quickly, and suddenly we were seniors. Then, on April 12, 1945, an announcement came over the loud speakers that President Roosevelt had died. As he was the only president we had ever known, everyone in the student body was deeply saddened. The hallways were lined with students and teachers alike, walking aimlessly around with tear-filled eyes. School was dismissed early and we each went sadly to our homes.

Then it was time to prepare for graduation. Our senior year was coming to an end. We had started during the war and would be ending our high school days with the war still in progress, although winding down. Our graduation ceremony was held in the auditorium where friends and relatives showered us with lei. I will always remember those three very happy years, with great friends and teachers. Now it was all over.

With high school behind me, I worked at a couple of jobs before becoming a hostess for Hawaiian Airlines flying on DC-3s, the last of the propeller planes. I left in 1947 to marry Alex Williams, who was attending Fred Archer's School of Photography in Los Angeles. After he graduated, we returned to Hawai'i when Alex took over his family business, Williams Photography, which his grandfather had acquired in 1883 from Menzies Dickson. We built a house in Niu Valley where we raised our three sons. Alex passed away in 1988 and our son, Matt, continues to run the family business.

*Grandmother holding Lorraine and
cousin and father sitting beside them*

*Lorraine beside her mom with
baby brother in Mom's arms*

*Lorraine with Outrigger Canoe
Club paddling crew mates*

SCHOOL DAYS

Waikiki beach was surrounded by barbed wire for the duration of the war

Dancing at lunchtime on the patio

On the way to Wahiawā to work in the pineapple fields

Working in the pineapple fields

Football team crammed into old school truck on the way to the "Termite Palace"

Students lined up for an afternoon football game at the "old termite palace"

Roosevelt's "Rough Riders" playing at Honolulu Stadium

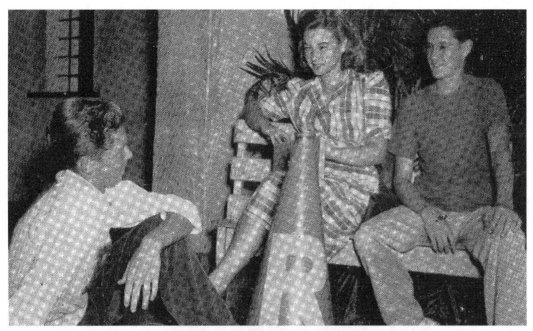

Mac Hill, Jane Steen and Tex Hays

Cheering the football team on from the top row at Honolulu Stadium

Mrs. Wise, school counselor

William Jennison taught classes while stationed on campus

Roosevelt principal Robert Spencer taking leave in 1945

Alice Nicholson, acting principal

*Kau Kau Korner, a popular hangout was the usual destination
after a Saturday night date*

*Benson Smith Drugstore at the corner of Fort and King Streets,
was a popular gathering place to hang out after school*

DEXTER DICKSON

My mother was born on the island of Kauaʻi; my Father was born on Oʻahu. My maternal grandmother, Louisa Kala, was pure Hawaiian, the granddaughter of Chief Kainoahou, a son of Kaumualiʻi, the last king of Kauaʻi. She married Charles Gay, whose family came from Scotland, via New Zealand, on their own three-masted sailing ship, *Bessie*, in 1863, when Charles was not yet two years old. After settling in Hawaiʻi, my great grandmother, Elizabeth Sinclair, bought the island of Niʻihau from Kamehameha III for $10,000 in gold; her daughters purchased large tracts of land on the island of Kauaʻi.

My mother, Amelia Gay, was the oldest of twelve children of Louisa Kala and Charles Gay. She attended Punahou School, and at the age of fifteen, taught English to Hawaiian children on Kauaʻi. In 1902, when her father, Charles Gay, purchased a large ranch above Kōele, on the island of Lānaʻi, she and most of the family moved to the small island. She was nineteen at the time; the younger siblings boarded at Punahou. Charles Gay was the first one to plant pineapple on Lānaʻi and the ranch was eventually acquired by Hawaiian Pineapple Co.

William Alfred Dickson, my father, was born in 1884, the son of Menzies Dickson, a photographer who lost a leg in the Civil War. Originally from Massachusetts, Menzies moved to Hawaiʻi not long after the war and was a familiar sight around Honolulu, riding his horse everywhere, even into bars. He owned and operated a photography business which he sold to J. J. Williams, an employee, in 1880. (Renamed Williams Studio, the business continues to this day, owned by the great grandson of J.J. Williams.) Menzies married Mary Kamaeleihiwa Miner, whose mother, Kalua, died in childbirth when Mary was born. She was raised by an aunt, Hamanalau. Kalua's father, Palea, was a great attraction at the now defunct Lalani Village in Waikīkī. He lived to be more than 100 years old. In his later years, Menzies became a rancher at Mokulēiʻa.

My paternal grandparents had three children: my father William, and two older daughters: Mabel, who died in early childhood, and Irene who married Evelyn Woods Low, son of the famous cowboy from Parker Ranch, Eben Low. Irene and her father-in-law were the ones who started the annual Kamehameha Day Parade.

My parents met when my father was working on Lānaʻi as bookkeeper for the Gay ranch. They had five children of their own; the eldest was Cecil Menzies, then Mary Louise, Ynez, Wilbur and I. Mom and Dad also became *hānai* parents of a cousin two years older than I, Roy

Gay, whose mother died in childbirth. I knew Roy as my true brother. Of the four boys and two girls in the family, I was the youngest. My family moved from Lānaʻi to Oʻahu before I was born and lived on Wilhelmina Rise.

Five years after my grandfather, Menzies Dickson, passed away my widowed grandmother, Mary, remarried. Her second husband was Cecil Brown, also born on Kauaʻi, who was a prominent attorney and legislator under the monarchy, and also served as Attorney General. Mr. Brown owned a great deal of land and wanted to sell some of it. He made a deal with my father that if he would sell three parcels in a country area called Makaua, Mr. Brown would give him a parcel of his own. Makaua was, and still is, a sparsely settled area between Kaʻaʻawa and Kahana Bay. Dad sold four parcels and thus became the owner of a large piece of property that consisted of many acres…I'm not sure how many, but it stretched from the mountains to the sea.

With some helpers, my father built a large house on the property on the *mauka* side of Kamehameha Highway. There was a spacious lawn in front, and directly across the highway was the ocean. The house had a concrete floor and *lānai* that stretched around two sides. The large living room was furnished with two huge *pūneʻe*. In back of the house, was a bunkhouse big enough for six beds, where company often slept.

There was no running water or electricity; however, there was a well in the front yard from which we pumped water into a large tank in the back of the house. From there, it was pumped into another tank above the bunkhouse. Beneath that tank was a shower with a pipe that ran from the tank to the bar-b-cue pit; when we wanted hot water, we lit a fire in the pit which warmed the pipe and the water in it. Our electricity came from twenty-five or thirty automobile batteries charged by a generator.

Dad turned part of our property into a ranch and farm where we raised vegetables and animals, including horses, pigs, chickens, ducks, and pigeons. As soon as we kids were old enough, we had chores to do, such as feeding and watering the animals, and picking vegetables.

Both of my parents worked in Honolulu; Mom was a teacher at Kaʻiulani School in Pālama, and Dad worked in the First Circuit Court before transferring to the City & County Building Department.

When we were old enough for school, we all traveled over the *pali* to Honolulu. My two sisters went to Punahou, and my brother, Cecil, went to McKinley. I started out at Lincoln Elementary, and then entered the seventh grade at Stevenson, the old Normal School, which had been turned into an English Standard intermediate school. Dad drove the family to work and school every day and picked us up afterwards for the long drive home. On the way, we often stopped for groceries at Ah Lin Market in Kāneʻohe, and we bought our poi at Waiāhole Poi Factory on Kamehameha Highway. Once we got home, we did our chores before anything else. Saturday was slaughter day, as well as harvest day. The fresh produce and meat were sold to Ah Lin Market.

On weekends, when we weren't doing chores on the farm, we spent our time in the ocean. We had a small row boat and went fishing, mostly for squid which were abundant in the water there. In those days, *konohiki* rights were still observed, which meant that only people from the area could catch squid there. The same applied to other areas such as Kahana Bay, where there were great schools of *akule*, but only the people of Kahana were allowed to catch them. When the schools were very large at Kahana, we were invited to participate in a *hukilau* in the bay. All the *akule* that were caught went to market. The *mullet, weke, pāpio*, and any other fish we caught in the net, were divided up among those who had helped.

Nearly every weekend we had lots of company; friends and relatives loved to come to the country and that kept Mother busy cooking. Her meals usually had plenty of raw and cooked fish, and of course, *poi*. Often the guests stayed over night and slept in the bunkhouse.

One weekend, in December of 1941, my brother Wilbur and I spent the weekend in town with my grandmother Gay, whose home was on the corner of Keʻeaumoku Street and Wilder Avenue. I remember there were several cousins there too. On Sunday morning we were awakened by really loud noises that sounded like explosions of some kind. We got up and went outside but couldn't see anything. Then we climbed up on the roof of the large two-story house and from there we could see dozens of planes in the distance, and lots of smoke, but mostly it was noise reverberating through the air that really startled us. After awhile, a neighbor came over and told us that Japanese were bombing Pearl Harbor. When we got over the initial shock, we climbed down from the roof and went back into the house to break the news to my grandmother. Before long, other relatives who lived closer to Pearl Harbor arrived and spent several days with us until they felt it was safe to return to their homes.

A lot of changes soon went into effect; martial law was declared, blackout and curfew were strictly enforced, and there were shortages of all kinds. The one that affected our family most was the gasoline shortage. It became impossible to continue the daily commute to and from the country, so my father hired someone to take care of the farm and we spent the rest of the war years in town, living with an aunt in Moanalua Valley.

When school started again several months later, I went to Roosevelt, the only English Standard High School in Hawaiʻi. The campus was surrounded by barbed wire because part of it was taken over by the Navy.

At Roosevelt, I found many of my old buddies from Lincoln and Stevenson, including Roy Perreira and Frank Dower. I joined the football team and played center for the Rough Riders. I loved football, and it was more important to me than school work. The first year I was on the team it was pretty sad; we tied Kamehameha, but lost every other game. Then our coach, "Babe" Webb, resigned, which made it even worse.

The next year everything changed. ʻIolani, a boys' school in Nuʻuanu, famous for its outstanding football teams, closed down for the duration of the war because so many of its students and teachers were drafted into the military. Roosevelt was lucky to get most of its players. A story August "Auggie" Reiman told was that he and a bunch of ʻIolani football players were standing on a corner waiting for Al Minn, another ʻIolani boy, to pick them up and take them to McKinley High School to register. Before he arrived, a truck, driven by Nathan Napoleon, a former Stevenson student who was on his way to register at Roosevelt, drove up and asked them where they were going. When they explained, Nathan said, "Hey, you guys don't want to go to McKinley. Come with me to Roosevelt, they have cuter girls!" So that, supposedly, is the inside story of how Roosevelt got its championship football team.

Among the ʻIolani players who played for the Rough Riders that second year were Nathan's brother, Walter Napoleon, Lunalilo Taylor, August Reimann, Harris Moku, Ralph Villiers, Edwin Fuller, Alfred Guigni, and Richard Hanchett. They joined starting quarterback, Charles "Spike" Cordeiro, George Hong, Stanley Alama, and other stalwart players to form a great team. The new coach was one of the best in the league, Jimmy Blaisdell, who was named "Coach of the Year" twice. One of the team's biggest victories was a 51 – 0 win over McKinley. I often wonder what that score would have been if Al Minn had got to the corner before Nathan.

Jimmy Blaisdell did not return the next year but we did have a good replacement in Jonah Wise. However, as many of our best players had graduated, we didn't have the same caliber team as the year before. In fact, the only victory we managed to eke out was against Punahou, but since they were our biggest rival, it was a sweet victory. We ended up in a tie with Kaimukī High, a brand new school.

The games were played in the old stadium on King Street in Mōʻiliʻili, called "The Termite Palace." We got there crammed into an old school truck. Win or lose, after every game, the *wāhine* would rush out onto the field to place a *lei* around our necks and give us a kiss. We walked off smothered with fragrant blossoms, white ginger being my favorite. Then afterward, there was always a party…sometimes more than one. Despite the blackout and curfew, we managed to have a great time. The parties I remember most are those at the Napoleon brothers' home on Punchbowl, and at Blondie Boyd's home on Lusitana.

Throughout my years at Roosevelt, our school counselor, Nina Wise, was an inspiration to all of us. She was a tall, stately woman whom everyone admired and someone you could go to for advice or help. However, if you cut class or played hooky, she could be really tough. I know that for a fact, as some buddies and I decided to hang out downtown one day instead of going to school. We were caught and suspended for a week. Mrs. Wise was strict, but fair, and we could tell she was truly concerned about our well-being.

On Mondays, as part of the war effort, we all went to Wahiawā to work in the pineapple fields. We boarded an old truck with seats lined up in the back and made the otherwise boring drive fun by telling jokes and singing songs. Once we got there, we really had to work hard. Dressed in heavy clothes, including shirts with long sleeves, we were hot and sweaty, slaving away in the hot sun. I also worked in the campus Victory Garden in which we grew carrots, beets, onions, lettuce, and other vegetables. The food we harvested was given to the school cafeteria. Since fresh produce was hard to come by during the war, it made the meals a lot tastier and more nutritious as well.

On school days, when not in class, working in the Victory Garden, or at football practice, I hung out with the other football players. They were a great bunch of guys and we have remained life-long friends. After much deliberation, I decided to quit school in my senior year and join the Merchant Marine, along with several other classmates. I was sorry to miss graduation, but have always felt myself a part of the class of '45 and my years at Roosevelt a very special part of my life.

In 1945 I joined the Merchant Marine and sailed on the USS Hannibal Victory. After the war, I came home and went to work for the City & County Building Department as a safety inspector. I met Vernadetta Amoka, a Kamehameha Schools graduate, in December of 1947 and we married the following year. We have four children, eight grandchildren, thirteen great-grandchildren, and five great great-grandchildren. When I retired from the C&C after more than thirty-three years, I started a banana farm, selling to both grocery stores and schools. For many years I was involved with FFA (Future Farmers of America), Hawaiʻi Young Farmers' Association, Hawaiʻi Farm Bureau, and the Lions Club of Kahaluʻu. I participated in fundraising for my son's canoe club, Keahiakahoʻe, mostly cooking kalua pig. When Verna passed away in 2008, we had been happily married for over fifty-nine years.

*Grandparents Louisa
Kala & Charles Gay*

*Mother second from left, father on right
Standing with an aunt & uncle.*

ELIZABETH HIRONAKA RATHBURN

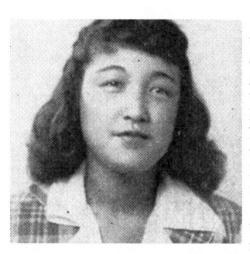

My maternal grandmother, Elizabeth Pa'awela, was pure Hawaiian and graduated in the first class at St. Andrews Priory. When she was about twenty, grandmother had a child out of wedlock. Her mother was very disappointed and upset, and sent her to Moloka'i to have the child; thus my mother was born. Not long after, her mother ordered grandmother back to Honolulu to go to work, but the child remained on Moloka'i with her father's family until she was nearly six years old.

After her mother passed away, grandmother got up the courage to go back to Moloka'i to ask for the return of her daughter. Her wish was granted and she brought my mother, also named Elizabeth, back to Honolulu and entered her in St. Andrew's Priory where she was raised by the nuns, rarely if ever, coming home for weekends or even vacations. The nuns taught her to play the piano and she became quite an accomplished musician. She graduated from the Priory in 1922. Grandmother later married John Wailehua, but the marriage was brief as he died not long after; she never re-married.

In those days, not too many people owned a car, so some of mother's high school classmates, who had met a car salesman, encouraged mother to date him so they could all ride in his car. That's how she met her future husband, a McKinley High School graduate named Denichi "Dan" Hironaka, My parents married after she graduated from the Priory and later they had four children. There were three girls: my sister Laola, me, Lydia, and my brother, Leonard.

My father was born November 18, 1899, one of five children. His parents lived in Mō'ili'ili; I remember they had a huge grape vine in their yard. We saw our paternal grandparents, probably not more than once a year.

We lived in Pearl City, which was a really small, country town at the time. On the main street, Lehua Avenue, was the Post Office, a grocery store, fire department, the court house, and Pearl City Tavern. Then there were four other streets, First, Second, Third, and Fourth, that branched off of Lehua. We lived at one end of First Street, and at the opposite end was the Police Station. On one of the streets was a small dairy farm with a gigantic banyan tree; we loved to climb up the branches and swing from the roots.

Just beyond Fourth Street were the railroad tracks which separated Pearl City from the Peninsula. In the middle of the Peninsula was a market owned and operated by the Ho family. It was the only store on the Peninsula and I often rode my bike there to buy groceries. Along the way was a fresh water spring in someone's yard with a pump that gushed water into a natural pool. It was freezing cold, but friends and I often went swimming there, although we probably weren't supposed to. At the end of the Peninsula was a ferry that went to Pearl Harbor, but you needed a pass to board. Pan Am planes were headquartered right next to it.

On the Peninsula there were many vacation houses that belonged to well-to-do people from Honolulu. They often spent weekends there and most of them had boats which they sailed around the harbor. We never got to meet any of them.

Our house was located on a large piece of property that we rented from friends. It was on two levels, with our house located on the upper one. A stone wall went completely around the spacious front yard where lots of mango trees and hibiscus bushes flourished. A sour sap tree grew at the entrance. Grandmother lived in a smaller house in the back and there was also a bathroom in a separate building…not an outhouse by any means, but a real bathroom with a tub, toilet, and basin in which to wash clothes. We raised chickens and always enjoyed fresh eggs for breakfast. We also had geese and a monkey that was attached to a wire in one of the trees. We couldn't play with him as he was mean and would bite us if we got too close. My father somehow came across him and bought him for fifty dollars. On the lower level of the property was a taro patch, mango and banana trees, and a thicket of bamboo. Below that was a river that flowed into Pearl Harbor.

We had a row boat and often paddled down the river to catch Samoan crabs by dropping a round net into the water. Then we'd pull up the net and take the crabs home to cook and eat. We lived very close to Pearl Harbor and often went clamming there. We waded in the mud, sticking our hands into the slimy goo until we'd find a clam which we'd put in a pail. When the pail was full, we'd go home, put the clams in a pot of boiling water, and when the shells popped open, we'd eat them.

My father worked a lot of overtime selling cars, and when he wasn't working, he hung out with friends so we rarely saw him; when he was home he was very stern and strict. But mother was always there, a wonderful, gentle, patient and kind person. She didn't work until I was out of high school when she became a kindergarten teacher. I remember her playing the upright piano we had in our living room, and occasionally she gave piano lessons.

We didn't leave the country very often but there was a special occasion in 1935 when our whole family drove to Honolulu to see Shirley Temple when she made an appearance at 'Iolani Palace. The grounds were crowded with thousands of people, mostly children with their parents, hoping to get a glimpse of their favorite movie star. I remember sitting on my father's shoulders as Shirley appeared on the second floor *lānai*. She must have been standing on a platform as we were able to see her as she waved at us and we all waved back.

When it was time for school, I spent the first two years in Pearl City, and then transferred to August Ahrens School in Waipahu, an English Standard School. We rode the bus to and from school. Before catching the bus home, we stopped at a little country store across the street to buy flavored ice cubes for two cents each, and sucked them on the ride home. August Ahrens went only to the sixth grade, so after that, mother decided I should go to Stevenson Intermediate, also an English Standard school. To gain admittance, an oral exam was required. I didn't pass, so mother went to speak with the principal. I'm not sure what she told him, but I was accepted. The school was located in Makiki, quite far away from our home. I took the bus when my father wasn't available to drive me. My older sister, Laola, went to Kamehameha. Lydia and my brother followed me to Roosevelt, but Leonard only spent a year there before joining the army.

The bus rides to school were fun, since the bus stopped in ‘Ewa, Waipahu, Pearl City, and Aiea, taking on all the country students going to school in Honolulu. We made friends with lots of them.

In 1941 I was in the eighth grade at Stevenson when, one Saturday night in December, we had a party at our house. Early the next morning, my mother, siblings and I, as well as some neighbors, were in our back yard talking about the party the night before. Suddenly a plane zoomed overhead, and we could see a round, red, ball under the wings. We didn't think much of it and kept on talking. Then another plane came flying over, and this time we could see bullets zipping through the air. The plane came so low I could actually see the pilot's face. At this moment, a neighbor came rushing out of his house, shouting loudly, "O‘ahu is being attacked." We ran into the house and found a bullet in the couch and another in the refrigerator. I dove under the sofa, scared to death. After awhile we thought to turn on the radio. "This is the real McCoy!" Webley Edwards, the announcer, kept repeating. "This is the real McCoy!" The bombs being dropped over Pearl Harbor made a horrendous noise as they fell. After a while, Mother decided we should leave for a safer place, so during a brief lull, we ran up the hill on Waimanu Home Road and watched the inferno from there. It was unbelievable! Smoke and flames everywhere. Fortunately, I wasn't old enough to comprehend the catastrophe. To me, it was more like an exciting adventure.

My father had not been home the night before, having attended a stag party in a friend's basement. They had been gambling and drinking, and finally went to sleep. It wasn't until they came out two days later that they learned the devastating news of the attack.

Later that day we were evacuated to August Ahrens School where we remained for nearly two weeks. All we had were blankets, pillows, and a very meager supply of food. After what seemed forever, we were allowed to return to our homes. Oh, how good it felt to sleep in my own bed again!

With the onset of the war, schools closed for several months, busses stopped running, rationing began, mail was censored, and everything as we knew it changed completely. Martial law went into effect almost immediately with a curfew and blackout strictly enforced. Within a few months, we were issued gas masks which we had to carry with us at all times.

My sister Laola and I, and the Austen sisters, Kanani and Roselani, went to USO dances in ‘Ewa where Mother and Mrs. Austen volunteered as chaperones. One night Robert Stack and Robert Taylor, who were in the military, came to the dance and the girls went crazy over them.

When school resumed in May, I returned to Stevenson where I finished the ninth grade before transferring to Roosevelt. Most of my Stevenson friends were also at Roosevelt, so the adjustment to a new school was easy. Susan Johnson and I became friends, and since she lived in Kapahulu, I often spent the night at her house rather make the long trip back to Pearl City, especially since there was very little transportation after dark. On weekends, Francis Siu and I frequently met at her home in Kalihi and took the bus to Waikīkī Beach to spend the day swimming and playing in the waves…this was after openings were made in the barbed wire that surrounded the beaches and access to the ocean was allowed.

My mother was meticulous about keeping our yard neat, and raked the leaves every day. When a fairly good sized pile accumulated, she would start a fire to get rid of them. One night after the family had gone to bed, a fire Mother had lit earlier in the day accidentally reignited. With blackout strictly enforced, the air-raid wardens, military police, and of course the neighbors, all came rushing to the scene. They arrived just as Mother rushed out of the house with a pail of water and dumped it on the fire. In her panic, she forgot that she was stark naked! Nobody said anything, but I guess the military police were convinced we weren't spies.

Fortunately, our family never experienced much prejudice because of our Japanese ancestry. However, there was an instance when my sister, Laola, a beauty queen at the University, went to a dance with a Naval man at an Officer's Club. Another beauty queen and her officer-date were with them. When some of the women and wives complained because they appeared to be Japanese, they were quietly asked to leave. We always thought it wasn't because of their race, but because they were by far the prettiest girls there.

In Pearl City, and other parts of the island, temporary camps were set up out among the bushes and trees. Somehow, there was an organ there in the open field and on Sunday, church services were held. One day an Army Captain came to our house and asked my mother if she would play the organ for the service. She agreed and Laola and I accompanied her to turn the pages. We remember the Captain as being a very nice person and were sorry to hear he was killed in the war.

One summer I worked at the Dole Pineapple Cannery with eight of my Roosevelt classmates. Our job was to stand at an assembly line, and as the pineapples passed by, pull an apparatus down that cored them. Most of the other workers were older and very serious about their jobs; we teenagers spent the time telling jokes and laughing so loud we nearly got fired.

Occasionally, I rode the train home to Pearl City, and often was the only civilian in my compartment. The rest were mostly sailors returning to their ships at Pearl Harbor. They really enjoyed talking to a civilian, especially a girl, and I enjoyed talking to them. I remember a Naval officer once smiling and nodding to me, and only years later did I realize he was probably thanking me for talking to the enlisted men and cheering them up.

One day, not long before the war ended in 1945, I was walking along the street in Pearl City when I heard the steady drone of plane engines. I looked up and was amazed to see hundreds of bombers flying by, really high in the sky. On and on they came, as I, and everyone else on the street, stood flabbergasted. For about ten minutes the sky was filled with large planes, blocking out even the sunlight. Although we never knew for sure, we assumed they were on their way to bomb Japan.

Another day I was sitting around at home with some friends when we heard the sound of huge explosions coming from Pearl Harbor. We rushed outside where the noise was deafening, and thick, black smoke was billowing above. We were scared to death that we were being attacked again. We ran down the railroad tracks about a half mile toward West Lock where we could look directly at the inferno; it was the most horrendous sight I've ever seen. Whole bodies and limbs were shooting up in the sky, then dropping back into the ocean. Flames were everywhere. Dozens of ships were on fire, those that weren't headed out to sea. Fire boats and tugs appeared on the scene with hoses but fires kept burning. Sirens shrieked as ambulances and trucks arrived to pick up dead and wounded bodies. Although we didn't stay until it was over, the noise and smoke continued until well after dark. We waited for the newspaper the next day to learn what had happened, expecting headlines to feature the story. Instead, there was a tiny article about "an insignificant fire with a few casualties at Pearl Harbor. We never found out what happened, although rumors floated around the neighborhood that it was sabotage or a Japanese suicide mission. (Just a few years ago the story was declassified and the cause of the terrible event made public. Unbelievably, it was caused by careless smokers working with ammunition aboard ships. Hundreds of lives had been lost, and hundreds injured; millions of dollars in Navy ships and war materiel were destroyed.)

Despite all the war-related activity, and the restrictions, we went on with our lives as best we could. A special event was spending the weekend with classmates Eleanor Dias and Pat Knapp at Kawena Kippen's beach house at Ka'awa. Rather than go to the beach, however, we sat around and played cards...usually canasta. Classmate Tim Monroe, who lived next door, sometimes joined us.

During football season, I never missed a game. We never paid to get into the stadium as the uncle of one of my classmates was a ticket collector and he let us in for free. We won the championship in 1944. Sadly, my one experience with racial prejudice involved one of our football players who came up to me one day and said, "If your name wasn't Hironaka, I'd ask you out." As he was a really cute guy, I was both stunned and flattered.

I didn't get a chance to do a lot of the things that my classmates did after school as I had to catch the bus for the long ride to Pearl City. The buses were always crowded with servicemen and I often had to wait while several packed buses passed by. Nevertheless, my high school years were a fun time, with one exception. Every Monday we went to the pineapple fields to work. Those of us who lived in the country were picked up along the highway, rather than having to go into town. I was always the last one on the truck as it headed out to Wahiawā for a day of hard labor in the hot sun.

I wasn't a very good student at Roosevelt, but managed to get through the three years and graduate. There was always so much going on and so many things to do, those studies seemed to take a back seat. I made the swim team and swam in the relay races. I remember one swimming meet in particular, held at the University of Hawai'i pool. We were confident of winning but someone managed to break out of her lane and we were disqualified. Those high school days were very good and happy years and when we graduated, although it was a joyful event, it made me sad to think that it was all over. Many of the friends I made there are still close friends today.

In the summer of 1945, I got a job with Morrison-Kneudsen, an international civil engineering and construction company that built Tripler Hospital. After a couple of years, I went to work for the State Tax Office. There I was reunited with Roosevelt classmates, Pat Phillips and Kawena Kippen. We remained life-long friends. I met my husband, Leroy G. Rathburn in 1948. He had served in the Navy during World War II and was attending the University of Hawai'i as a civil engineering student. He graduated in 1950 and went to work for the Board of Water Supply. In September of 1950, Leroy received a phone call from the Navy Reserve at Pearl Harbor informing him that he was to be recalled in just one week. He had just seven days to clear up whatever he was doing and report to Pearl Harbor. The Korean War was in full swing when his ship was sent there. So in just a week, we decided to get married. He was gone for two years and I worked at the Tax Office until he returned. When the war was over, we traveled frequently to San Francisco, our favorite city. We had two children, a boy and a girl. Our daughter lives in California but visits frequently. Our son passed away early, while attending the University of Puget Sound. Leroy retired in 1984 and passed away in 2011. I now live at a retirement home, One Kalākaua, and keep active with my sister and friends, many my high school classmates.

*Mother playing organ for soldiers, sisters
Laola and Liz helping.*

*Grandmother,
Elizabeth Pa'awela*

JAMES BENJAMIN SEELIG

My story begins in Goldendale, Washington, where I was born on June 17, 1927. My birth name was James Irwin Van Hoy. I have an older sister and twin brothers, who were eighteen months younger than I. In 1932, when the country was suffering from the great depression, times were hard, jobs were scarce, and my parents divorced; I was five years old at the time. My mother was so poor she had to ask her landlady for milk. My father, without a job, couldn't help her financially as he was just as bad off as she. Finally, the courts stepped in and decided to send my brothers and me to an orphanage in Seattle. My sister, who suffered from a bone disease which affected her leg, remained with my mother. Not long after, my twin brothers were separated when they were adopted by different families, both living in Washington State.

I have only a few memories of life in the orphanage; one was of waking up in a crib with my hands tied to the rails, being fed ice cream. Apparently it was standard procedure when a boy has his tonsils removed and a circumcision performed. Another memory is getting caught spitting the castor oil they fed us each morning into the footlocker at the end of the bed. It started to leak out after several weeks.

How I ended up in Hawai'i is a long story. It goes back to World War I when my future adopted mother, Adria Ponzanela, worked in a shipyard in Seattle as secretary to the shipyard manager. As a young woman of twenty-three, she needed a safe place to live, and after searching the area, found a nice, small boarding house for young women, owned and operated by a woman named Mrs. Dickinson. Her son, Porter, eventually moved to Hawai'i where he became editor of the Honolulu Star Bulletin, one of O'ahu's two daily newspapers. In the meantime, my future mother moved to Hawai'i and married Ben Seelig, my adopted father. Porter Dickenson got to know the Seeligs and Adria asked if his mother would mind going to the orphanage to choose a child for them, as she could have no children of her own. I was almost six at the time. Most people who want to adopt a child want one that is under one year of age, but somehow I was chosen, and within a few days I was on a ship headed for Hawai'i.

The ship was the Matson Navigation Company's luxurious liner, the Lurline, where I was put in the charge of a ship employee. I was wandering around one afternoon and found a lit pipe that had been placed on the arm of a deck chair while the owner was playing shuffle board. It was hot to the touch, so trying to be a good citizen, I threw it overboard where it couldn't do any harm. Years later a family friend was visiting our home and commented that the last time he came to Hawai'i, some unscrupulous person had thrown his pipe off the ship.

Upon my arrival in Hawai'i, my new parents went to court to officially adopt me. They changed my name from James Irwin Van Hoy to James Benjamin Seelig. It was quite a traumatic change for me, to suddenly be part of a strange family, and it took a while for me to adjust. At first, I didn't trust anyone, but as time went on, things got better and I was very happy. Two years later, they adopted another boy named Frank.

Ben Seelig was born and raised in New York City. He was a stern man who brooked no nonsense from friend or foe. Dad moved to the Islands in 1919 and lived at the Elks Club until he married Adria in 1923. Dad worked as sales manager for Theo H. Davies where he remained until they wanted to move him to their Big Island office. This he refused to do, and subsequently resigned and opened his own business. He was a wholesaler for cigars, candy, and liquor. His claim to fame was that he introduced "Pink Champagne" to Hawai'i.

My mother's family came from Florence, Italy, and moved to Erie, Pennsylvania, when she was seventeen. She traveled around the world twice and was on a train in China that was held up by bandits. She later moved to Seattle, Washington, and then to Hawai'i when she was around twenty-eight. After she married my father and he opened his business, she ran the operation; he was the salesman, she was the boss. She drove a car like a man, and if someone cut her off, she used very loud language with words I never understood until I was twenty-two.

My parents lived in Mānoa Valley, in the same house that the Massie couple lived in before the famous rape case of 1931. Shortly after I arrived, they built their home in Kailua, which was then a sleepy, little, over-the-*pali* neighborhood. My father built the first year-round residence on Kailua Beach in 1923, on land purchased from the Castle Estate. Until then, all the houses in both Kailua and Lanikai, a small town which adjoined it, were strictly vacation homes. Right next door to our house was the old Kāne'ohe Ranch office, which later moved up to the foot of the Pali Road.

When I was growing up, there were only a few places of note. As you entered Kailua, after winding your way down the *pali,* there was Kailua Tavern, famous for the soft coconut meat served right out of the shell with the milk still in it. You drank the milk through a straw and then devoured the meat with a long-handled spoon. There was also Date Service Station on Kailua Road, the only place to buy gas, as well as a small grocery store. There were watermelon patches and the Campos Dairy for fun and entertainment. I learned to ride a horse at the dairy and once fell off right smack into a cow pie. Roy Campos was one tough dude, but his sisters were beautiful. Andy's Drive-in came along later, known for its delicious hot dogs.

Lanikai was another little neighborhood of beach cottages adjoining Kailua where movie stars and celebrities often rented vacation homes. On the other side of Kailua was Kāne'ohe, just a few miles away; the climate was different, and it rained a lot. There were papaya, banana, and taro farms, and it was a real agricultural and residential community. In between was a peninsula called Mōkapu, also consisting of vacation homes.

It was great living on the ocean with a nice sandy beach in our back yard. When I was older, I often went spear-fishing all day out by the reef. When I wasn't fishing, I was body surfing. My thoughts go back to the time when my folks would have BBQ's for about fifteen people; then in the evening they would all go skinny dipping. Today, you'd probably get arrested for doing that.

There were no schools then in Kailua, so my parents enrolled me in first grade at 'Iolani, a private boys' school in Nu'uanu, affiliated with the Episcopal Church. I have many memories of 'Iolani. My first grade teacher was named Miss Street and I was put into a class to learn tap dancing. What a fiasco! My most vivid memory of 'Iolani was the coconut tree that grew on campus. It was half way between the dining hall and the first classroom. The tree was about thirty feet high and in the middle of a circular pond. One afternoon someone climbed up the tree to get some coconuts. He twisted one off its stem then threw it to the ground below. Meanwhile, I was looking into the pond to see if there were any fish there when a coconut hit me on the top of the head, knocking me unconscious; I was out for about ten minutes.

Shortly after starting school I came down with polio in my right arm. Oddly, I was the only child in Hawai'i in 1933 that contracted the disease. After recovering at Shriner's Hospital, I returned to 'Iolani, and after skipping the fourth grade, continued through the eighth grade. Father Bray was the football coach and he was tough as nails. His players really admired him and he developed some great athletes; the school won the football championship year after year.

One of the highlights of my young life was playing with Shirley Temple when her family brought her to stay for a time at a beach-front home in Lanikai. They invited about fifteen kids from Kailua and Lanikai to come and play with her. She was about ten or twelve then. I found Shirley to be a quiet girl who smiled a lot. But Shirley Temple wasn't the only important person I met in my young life. When President Franklin Roosevelt visited the islands in 1935, he was touring the island in a convertible and saw me at the side of the road with my arm in a sling because of the polio. He stopped to say "hello" and pat my head.

When I finished the eighth grade, my parents sent me to a school in Santa Monica, California, with my 8th grade teacher, Mrs. Nunes, who was entering into a two-year teacher exchange program. They felt that a mainland school would be a good experience for me. I enjoyed going to school there, and played on the football team. While in the tenth grade, Pearl Harbor was attacked. When we heard the news, we thought it was a joke, but after awhile, listening to the radio announcer repeat the story over and over, we were convinced.

My parents where able to book me on a convoy heading back to Hawai'i. The convoy that took me from San Francisco to the Islands was comprised of three ships. It took six days as we zigged and zagged and ran without lights at night; I thought it was fun and exciting, but in retrospect it was pretty scary. I was sixteen years old and wanted to man one of the guns on the ship that protected it against enemy aircraft. The closest I got was to sit in the gunners chair for about twenty seconds.

Unfortunately I was not able to go back to 'Iolani as they had discontinued grades ten through twelve for the duration of the war. I was at a loss as to what I should do; finally I decided to go to Roosevelt.

My brother Frank went to Punahou, a private school, but I refused to go there, thinking that's where the wimps went. But when I dated a girl from there, I went to the Punahou carnival nearly every year. This was almost my undoing, as one year after the carnival was over, I decided to test the old Hawaiian *pali* pork theory. There was a legend that Madame Pele, the goddess of the volcano, and her large white dog, would get you if you took pork over the *pali* at midnight. I owned a surplus jeep that had been converted to a stretcher carrier. I took out the poles that supported the stretchers, leaving the passenger side empty. Then I went to the dump and found an old seat which I put in the jeep with a nice cushion from home. I saved some pork from the carnival, and at midnight, headed up the *pali*. The jeep had no roof so the wind was blowing over me as I rushed up the mountain. Suddenly, I felt something brush up my right leg. Needless to say, I was scared to death. All I could think was, "Pele is after me!" Oops, it was just the wind blowing the seat cushion onto my leg. Whew!

My two years at Roosevelt enabled me to meet some fine people. I remember Janice Hobson, Jack Myers, Charles Evensen, Vernon Chun, Bob Clarke, Nat Andrade, Wesley Walters and many others. I played on the football team as a line backer. The year I played, we won eight games and lost two.

Roosevelt was a great experience despite the war-time conditions; we worked in the pineapple fields on Monday and my job was mostly pulling weeds. We had to lug gas masks around everywhere, and the U.S. Navy took over part of the campus for the duration. However, I think it made our class closer, for all we went through.

I was looking forward to graduation but was drafted right out of the twelfth grade in my senior year so I didn't graduate with the class of 1945. The war ended just a few months later, but I was two credits short when drafted. After being discharged from the Army, I had to go to summer school in order to get my diploma. However, I'll always consider myself a part of the Class of '45.

After high school,l I was drafted and spent my service time at Schofield Barracks on O'ahu. My unit was saved from Guadalcanal duty when we were quarantined to the Barracks due to a measles outbreak. After the war, I went to Eastern Washington College of Education (now Eastern Washington University) in Cheney, Washington. After graduating in 1951 I returned to O'ahu and married my girlfriend, Suzanne Johnson.

We lived in Kailua where we raised our family of four boys and two girls. We divorced in 1975, and in 1988, Suzanne passed away. In 1951 I also went to work for Mutual Telephone Company (later Hawaiian Telephone Company) where I spent thirty-six years in sales and marketing, education and training. In 1976, I met Pat Orme and we were married in 1990. In 1993 we moved to Eugene, Oregon.

Jimmy and Frank with Mom

*Jimmy and younger
brother Frank*

Arriving on the Lurline

Georgia Schultz Rush

My parents met and fell in love during World War I, which is surprising since their homelands were fighting against each other at the time. My father, Jens Johannes Christian Schultz, was born in 1891 in Schleswig-Holstein, a city in Germany on the Baltic Sea near Denmark. His father was a tug boat captain who took his son, then in his early teens, along with him as part of the crew. Growing up around the shipyard, my father eventually became a qualified Marine Engineer. He joined the German Merchant Marine prior to World War I and traveled around South America and the Pacific Ocean. His ship visited all the German colonies, as well as Rapa Nui (Easter Island), Fiji, Kiribati (Christmas Island), and China, among others. His ship picked up merchandise made in China, but stamped "Made in Germany."

In 1914, his ship came to Honolulu to refuel. At the time, an English company, Theo. H. Davies, controlled the coal in Hawai'i and they refused to refuel a German ship as England and Germany were already engaged in World War I. Stranded for several months, my father jumped ship and got a temporary job as a mechanic with Schuman Carriage Co., the oldest car dealership in Hawai'i. After working there for a short time, he left for San Francisco, California, hoping to return to Germany. When he approached the German Consul, he was told to forget about returning to his homeland as Germany and the United States were about to go to war. He found a temporary job in San Francisco, and while working there, some friends introduced him to my mother; it was love at first sight.

My mother, Edith Sarah Eades was born in Marlborough, England, in 1886. Her father died after falling from a scaffold while glazing windows in the local church when mother was just an infant. When she was thirteen years old, her mother died, and Mother went to London to work as an "upstairs-downstairs" maid for a wealthy family on Cromwell Road. She became friends with a young woman who was working as a cook for the same family. They saved their money and embarked on an adventurous journey aboard the S.S. Laurentic, a ship of the White Star Line, to Quebec, Canada. From there, they traveled by train to Vancouver, British Columbia, then down to San Francisco where mother found a job taking care of the young daughter of the owners of Helwig's restaurant.

My parents married in San Francisco in 1918, and after the war, decided to make their home in Honolulu. Shortly after they arrived, my father got a job as an electrician with Von Hamm Young Co. Ltd., and worked there from 1919 until 1941. He taught himself to repair automobiles and was soon an accomplished mechanic. He became an American citizen in 1923, my mother in 1958.

My brother, Jens Robert Schultz, was born in 1920 in Honolulu. He attended St. Louis College, which was then located in downtown Honolulu, before moving to its present location in Kaimukī. He later went to Ali'iolani before graduating from Roosevelt High School in the class of 1939. He was employed by Hawaiian Electric Co. until he was drafted into the Army in 1945.

I was born in 1927 at Kapi'olani Maternity Home which was then located on Beretania Street near Kalākaua Avenue, close to the present Foodland Super Market. I was born on July 27, the birthday of a family friend named George, and because I also had an uncle named George, my parents named me Georgia Edith (after my mother) and my Hawaiian name, Imailani, was given to me by a family friend.

We lived in Kaimukī, first on Pāhoa Avenue, and then on Manini Way on Wilhelmina Rise. On the hill above our house were several carnation farms where the small, sweet pink carnations that you rarely see today were grown. There were lots of kids in our neighborhood, mostly boys, and we had fun playing games with improvised equipment. We fought battles using trash can lids for shields, walked around with milk cans attached to our feet with resin from *keawe* beans, played tag, snipped off ends of African tulip pods and squirted them at each other, and we even chopped tails off of geckos to see them wiggle. We strung covers from milk bottles from one tree to the next as radio receivers. On Halloween, we were very naughty and rolled garbage cans down Wilhelmina Rise, and soaped cars. We climbed into the storm drains along the roadside and pretended to be stuck, hailing the cars that drove by. If the cars stopped, we would giggle so the drivers knew we were just joking. We could even go through the pipes of the storm drains beneath the street from one side to the other.

One mother in the neighborhood had a car, and during summer vacations she often drove us to Waikīkī to swim in front of the Royal Hawaiian Hotel; on several occasions, she took us hiking up to Sacred Falls, on the North Shore near Hau'ula.

As it is today, Kaimukī was a residential neighborhood with most of Wai'alae Avenue occupied by stores and businesses. However, I don't think that any of the early stores remain. We had two theaters, the Kaimukī Theater and the Queen Theater. We purchased most of our groceries at L. Qwai Yow, located on the corner of Koko Head and Wai'alae; across the street was a tiny sushi shop that sold delicious cone sushi which contained thin strips of string beans and carrots; the price was three for ten cents. Kaimukī Dry Goods had great fabrics, and as many of us, or our mothers, sewed our clothes, their annual remnant sale was a big event with a long line waiting to get in. Hollisters Drug Store, located where First Hawaiian Bank is now, was famous for its hot fudge sundaes.

The street car started in Chinatown and went up Wai'alae Avenue; when it reached the end of the line at Koko Head Avenue, the conductor flipped the seats over so they faced the opposite direction. During my early school years, when we got to the end of the line, we either walked home or waited at the bottom of the hill for a ride with family or friends.

Mother usually shopped by phone, calling L. Quai Yow in the morning for groceries which would be delivered in the afternoon. If she wanted to shop in Kaimukī, she walked down the hill and took a taxi home, unless it was Saturday when she and Dad went shopping together. Then they frequently drove downtown to the Metropolitan Meat Market on King Street for cold cuts, smoked salmon and pickled herring. There was also the "vegetable man" who drove his truck through the neighborhood selling fresh fruits and vegetables in the morning.

No doubt because of his many years at sea, my father had a deep love for the ocean; he built several small boats and sailed the waters of Kāne'ohe Bay. He joined the Kāne'ohe Yacht Club in 1932 and it became an important part of our family life from then on. Each Sunday during racing season we went to the Yacht Club, which was then located in He'eia, across from Moku o Lo'e, now called Coconut Island. Mother packed a big picnic bag filled with the deli products from the meat market, along with bread, potato salad, and other goodies, and off we'd go, driving down the Pali Road with its sharp hairpin turns. Dad entered most of the races with his Spartan sailboat, and later, his M.P., and won many trophies over the years.

While the sailors were out racing in Kāne'ohe Bay, a few of us kids used the dinghy to row over to Coconut Island. At this time it was owned by the Territory of Hawai'i and was a much smaller island where the Sea Scouts often camped. In the late thirties, it was sold to Chris Holmes, the Fleishman Yeast heir, who dredged up sand and coral from the bay to enlarge the island to twice its size and developed it as a luxurious retreat for entertaining guests. He brought an old sailing vessel, the Seth Parker, to the island and cemented it into one of the piers and turned it into a party house. He also created a mini zoo with a baby elephant and monkeys, and even had a bowling alley built.

During the off season, when there were no races, the family went sailing out to the sand bar in the bay and swam and picnicked all afternoon. It was so peaceful and uncrowded. Also in the bay was Kekepa, also called Turtle Back Island, and Kapapa, above the sandbar, where there is an ancient fishing *heiau*.

There was a long pier that extended from the Yacht Club into the bay where the boats docked. We often went fishing there for *manini*, using fishing lines with *'ōpai* for bait. The *manini* were too tiny to eat, but mother cooked them and fed them to our cat. We also went into the water at the end of the pier, which was scary as it was way over our heads and I didn't know how to swim at the time.

There were several large *hau* trees growing around the old Yacht Club and we often climbed the branches and swung from one tree to another. Across the highway was a deep valley with freshwater pools fed by streams flowing from the mountains. A friend sometimes drove us up there to fish for swordfish, mollie, and rainbow fish, all little aquarium fish.

One Thanksgiving Day, my dad and I went over to the Yacht Club for a leisurely sail while mom stayed home to roast the turkey. Before the developers bulldozed the land around the bay, there were beautiful coral reefs with an abundance of fish, and that day the bay was very calm and glassy. Before long, we both dozed off and landed up on the reef. We had to pull up the center board to free the boat before we could head back to shore.

In 1939, Mother and I took a trip on the Matson ship, Lurline, to California to attend the World's Fair in San Francisco. After meeting some friends we visited Crater Lake in Oregon, and Mt. Lassen in northern California. It was my first trip to the mainland.

When I was older, Dad let me crew with him in races on his twenty-foot MP which, incidentally, was named "Georgia." Often, when the waters were rough and we were chilled by the spray of cold water, Dad would pass me a bottle of watered-down whiskey and I would take a sip or two to warm up. Once I entered a *wāhine* race with Dad's MP and somehow managed to capsize. Dad was humiliated and I never raced alone again.

Our first home on Manini Way had two large mango and two large avocado trees in the yard. (We called them alligator pears.) Oh! How we enjoyed the delicious fruit when they were in season! Christmas was just a small family affair as there were only my parents, my brother and I. After opening our gifts on Christmas Eve, we joined hands and gave a hearty rendition of "O Tannenbaum." Before going to bed, I hung one of my father's socks on my door knob and in the morning it was filled with goodies. I knew it was my mother who put them there, but I could never catch her at it. It was the same at Easter; the door bell would ring and I would open the door and there would be an Easter basket. I knew it was my brother who put it there, but he ran out of sight as fast as he could to hide.

Then one Saturday night in December of 1941, a friend spent Saturday night at our house. We were up early having fun, dancing around the house, listening to our favorite music on the phonograph, and enjoying a typical Sunday morning. Suddenly, my friend's mother came speeding up the hill, parked her car, and ran across the lawn, all excited, shouting, "The Japs are bombing Pearl Harbor. Turn on the radio!" She took her daughter and quickly drove away. Dumbfounded, we turned the dial to hear Webley Edwards, the KGMB announcer, say, in almost frantic tones, "We're not fooling, this is the real McCoy! The Japanese are attacking Pearl Harbor!"

After recovering from our initial shock, we all ran as fast as we could to the first reservoir on the side of Wilhelmina Rise where there was a panoramic view of Pearl Harbor. In awe, we watched as black smoke formed huge clouds across the sky. We could barely see the Japanese bombers as they dropped their deadly missiles onto ships that lay quietly at anchor. When we saw a plane fly over the McCully area, not too far away, and drop an incendiary bomb, we decided to go home and listen to the radio.

Governor Pointdexter immediately proclaimed martial law and a blackout and curfew were put into effect. When the radio fell silent, it was even scarier than the news. It was several hours before our only two stations came on again. Throughout the night, we sat, glued to the radio, unable to sleep, wondering what was coming next.

What came next for our family was a horrible shock. Early in the evening of December 8th, a big, black car drove into our driveway, and two large men in dark suits and hats got out of the car, walked up to the front door and rang the bell. My brother, who was in the living room, opened the door. One of the men said, "We're from the Immigration Department and want to see Jens Schultz." My brother didn't know what to make of it, but leaving the men standing on the doorstep, hurried into the kitchen where my parents were talking. "Dad," he said, "some men want to talk to you." My father walked into the living room, with me following behind. "We'd like you to come with us to answer some questions," one of the men said. When my father turned to go back to the kitchen to tell my mother, one of the men reached out and firmly took his arm. Standing behind him, I thought I saw a gun under his jacket and I was really frightened. I rushed to the kitchen to tell my mother what was happening but by the time we came back to the living room, my father was walking up the driveway, with a man on each side. They got into the car, my father next to the driver, and the other man in the back seat. Then down the hill and out of sight they went.

My brother, mother and I stood there, flabbergasted, not knowing what to think or do. What could we do? Just wait to see what happened. We heard from other German and Italian families that were in similar situations, and in another case, both parents were taken and two young children left alone. Finally reality set in and we accepted the fact that my father had been interned but we had no idea where they had taken him. Every day Mother sat by the window weeping, watching the convoys sailing to the mainland and wondering whether Dad was on one of the ships.

Christmas came and went along with New Year's, and finally, around the middle of February, we received a letter from my father expressing his great concern for us. He told us that he had been detained at the Immigration Station for four very unpleasant weeks. Now, he related, he was on Sand Island where things were much better. "I do not know," he wrote, "why I am detained here, as I have done nothing against our government, neither in words nor even in thought, that justifies the treatment I have received." We all wept when we read the letter, but immediately sat down to write him and assure him that we were fine but missed him very much. The internees were allowed to write one letter a week and to receive mail, but it was censored, and no news of the war or anything political was permitted. The men he was interned with were mostly Germans, and a few Italians. Although they lived in tents with simple cots for beds, life was bearable.

Meanwhile, we carried on as best we could. Practically all public services were shut down. Buses temporarily stopped running, mail wasn't delivered, and when it was, it was censored. All schools were closed for about four months. When they reopened, the students were sent to the nearest school. Since I lived on Wilhelmina Rise, I went to Ali'iolani for the afternoon session to complete the ninth grade.

Since our family was deprived of income, except for my brother's salary at Hawaiian Electric, I got a summer job working at Wall-Nichols, a stationary store, to help pay for my school books and clothes. The hourly wage was thirty cents an hour and, as I was underage, could only work thirty-five hours a week. Mother raised chickens in the back yard and earned a few dollars selling eggs. The chickens that stopped laying were butchered and used to help feed the family.

It was not until May of 1942 that families were allowed to visit their loved ones on Sand Island. We could hardly wait to see Dad, and when the day finally came, we assembled at Pier 11 with other eager families, and boarded a launch which shuttled us to the camp; oddly, we were not allowed to take our gas masks with us. Dad had lost several pounds but was in good health. The group was able to play volleyball, and Dad got to work in the machine shop where he made several wooden bowls from the wood of *kiawe* trees on the island. The food was great as several of the German chefs from the large hotels were also detained at the camp and they were the cooks.

My father always maintained that he was glad "this happened to me in the United States, rather than being an American in Germany." He was never a bitter man because of this experience.

When I went back to school, I had mixed feelings about exactly where I belonged. I felt different from the other students. The only one I shared by feelings with was a boy whose father was also detained on Sand Island. He attended another school and I only saw him on Sunday, or when we occasionally dated.

The transition from Stevenson Intermediate to Roosevelt High School was a big step for me. The social life, especially, was very enjoyable and I made many new friends. Although I became quite close to several, I was never able to confide in them about my private life, and they had no idea what I was holding back. It was simply too painful to talk about, although I do believe a couple of the teachers knew my secret.

I took mostly secretarial courses, including typing and shorthand. We had some great teachers, but my favorites were Miss Johnson, the chemistry teacher, and Miss Matthews, who taught history. All the teachers dressed very properly, and many were spinsters. In my freshman year, I had a part in the annual Roosevelt musical, formerly called "Hav-a-Laugh," which, because of the war, had been reduced to "Hav-a-Chuckle."

I was elected Homeroom Vice President and joined the Science and Shorthand Clubs. In my senior year, I was chosen to be a song leader, along with the Hopkins' sisters, "Peewee" and Jean, and Anita Campos.

After school, my friends and I often went to Waikīkī for surfing and swimming. I belonged to the Uluniu Women' Swim Club, which was located adjacent to the Outrigger Canoe Club in the heart of Waikīkī.. A favorite Friday night date was to attend "first vue" at the Waikīkī Theater, and then go to Kau Kau Korner for a hamburger and coke afterwards. It was a place where you ran into all your friends.

Every summer I got a job to help pay for my school supplies as we continued to struggle financially. One year I worked downtown at Patton's Stationary Store, another I spent typing at the Star Bulletin. Selling clothing at McInerney's was yet another source of summer income.

After eighteen months on Sand Island, Dad was finally released. What a joy it was to have him home again! We celebrated quietly at home. Dad was able to return to his former job at Von Hamm Young and eventually opened his own electrical repair shop.

Our senior year came much too quickly. I had mixed emotions...sorry to be leaving Roosevelt, yet looking forward to getting out in the world and finding a job, as my parents couldn't afford to send me to college. The graduation ceremony was a tearful affair but the dinner and dance afterward at Hawaiian Town, a night club on Kapiʻolani Boulevard, was great fun. To attend, we had to have a special permit obtained from the Honolulu Police Department as war restrictions were still in place. It was just one of the many inconveniences we were used to. And so we danced the night away and the next morning, woke up to a new phase in our lives.

When my husband, Dwight Rush, Roosevelt Class of 1946, passed away in 2009, we had been married for over fifty years. We had wonderful adventures traveling the road of life with its humps and bumps, and what a grand time we had for the most of it. I ended up with four wonderful children, nine grandchildren, and so far, one great grandson. We traveled to Europe and visited my parents' homelands in England and Germany and enjoyed several trips to places in the south Pacific, including Tahiti, Ponape, Palau, Tonga, and the islands of New Guinea. We also did a lot of camping in places like the Nāpali Coast on Kauai and the island of Molokaʻi. I still keep in touch with some very dear classmates. The best of these memories I cherish every day.

Georgia as a song leader

Mom, brother Jens, Georgia

Georgia sailing on Kaneohe Bay

Quai Lum Young D.D.S., M.S.P.H.

My paternal grandfather, Sam Choy Young, was born in 1851, the twenty-first generation of his family, in Sam Heurn Village, Panglarn County, China. He emigrated to Hawai'i in the early 1850s. My paternal grandmother, Loo Jook, was born in 1878 and came to Hawaii at the age of thirteen from Hah Chuck Village, also in Panglarm County. They married when she was eighteen. Grandfather later became an herbalist who grew green, heart-shaped leaves called *lau eep*, which he shipped to China and the mainland in wooden crates lined with *ti* leaves. My grandmother served as a Buddhist Priestess at the Kwan Yin Temple on Vineyard and River Streets in downtown Honolulu. As kids, we loved to visit her at the Temple because she often gave us her loose change, such as nickels, dimes, and sometimes a quarter. Wow, it made us kids feel rich!!

My father's sister, Kam Oot Young, married Lum Wah Hin in Honolulu in 1921. He started the Honolulu Broom Factory next door to his father's grocery store on Vineyard Street. Both businesses prospered; it was there I had my first and only ride on the back of a large turtle that was caught by several employees of Uncle Lum. The Salvation Army Band played in front of Uncle Lum's father's grocery store every Sunday evening and we tossed coins against the brass drum to watch them bounce. There was also a short service for the wayward and those who needed help. During my growing-up years, I spent a lot of time at the broom factory and grocery store with my six cousins. My father, Kwon Leong Young, was third of the six children of Sam Choy and Loo Jook Young and was born in Honolulu. When his mother took the rest of the family to China, he was raised by his father. Father attended formal school only through grade seven, but continued to pursue higher learning through adult courses at the University of Hawai'i. He received the Chinese Parent of the Year Award and the coveted Navy E Award, the highest government award for a civilian. He attended the University of Hawai'i for thirty years without ever getting a degree.

My maternal grandfather, Wai Sing Chang, was descended from a family of educated scholars, accountants, merchants, and herbalists. After high school, he went to Shanghai to study classical history and literature, mathematics, accounting, and English.

Wai Sing unexpectedly received a letter from his bother-in-law, Nim Yuen, asking him to come to Hanapēpē, Kaua'i, to be an accountant for his rice plantation. In true Chinese tradition, he took a wife before departing to a foreign land. In 1887, he married Ah Jook Shee whose father was a dyer of cloth and supervisor of the dye department in a textile factory. The brother-in-law, Nim Yuen, on whose rice plantation my grandfather went to work, had a Hawaiian wife named Kalanikau Namohala, who was from the island of Niʻihau. Thus we had several part-Hawaiian cousins.

Grandmother Jook Shee's feet were bound in early childhood, in keeping with ancient tradition required for females of middle and upper social strata. As she was trained in the social graces of Chinese etiquette, Chinese families in Hanapēpē depended on Grandmother Chang to teach their daughters proper etiquette for their weddings. She was a patient and soft-spoken woman.

Wai Tsing and Jook Shee had four sons, two of whom became dentists, and two who became medical doctors. Their three daughters included my mother Mildred, and her sisters Florence, and Frances, who married Leonard Kahakanui Fong, City and County Auditor for Honolulu for thirteen years, and a fixture at Kūhiō Park. Their son, Bernard, became a physician specializing in internal medicine. He is six months older than I, and I credit him with teaching me how to drive, play the ʻukulele, and drink beer. I did him a similar favor many years prior, by getting us both kicked out of Chinese language school.

My mother, Mildred Ngit Sim (Chang) Young, was born in Hanapēpē in 1898. She was a talented seamstress and made all of our clothing, some from bleached rice sacks. She quit school early in order to work and send money to her brothers for their education. She was kind and understanding mother to her seven offspring. Mother was very knowledgeable about most things, as she read a lot and instilled in us a strong desire to learn.

I was the oldest of the children, born on December 15, 1926 in Honolulu at Queen's Hospital. We lived on Hotel Street at the time, on what are now the State Capitol grounds. Times must have been difficult in the late 1920's and early 1930's. I remember not being able to take a bath because my dad and his friends were making some red liquid in the bathtub (wine?). I also recall the only time I saw my mother cry, because all she could feed us was sugared water for several days. At the age of five, I entered the first grade at Royal School, but because I suffered from asthma during my early years, I was absent quite often..

In the 1930's, my dad bought a lot in Kaimukī on Paʻahana Street, and built a two-story home with a separate garage. The home is still there, in spite of the termites. We had a good life in that multi-racial neighborhood which consisted of a Japanese family with a wonderful garden, the Shaws and their three children who were Irish and Portuguese, a German family, the Hagens, as well as the Gumphers who were German-Hawaiian. Then there were the Brancos, of Portuguese descent, an English explorer named Plummer, a Samoan family, and a pure Hawaiian family named Pali. Our next-door neighbors, the Evans, were from the Pacific Northwest.

Father designed and supervised the construction of our house with the help of a Japanese friend. He devised one of the first solar water heaters in Hawaiʻi with copper pipes on the roof, enclosed with glass and an insulated storage tank built inside the chimney.

After we moved, I repeated the first grade at Liholiho Elementary School. My teacher, Mrs. Abreu, a strict part-Hawaiian lady, often lined up five of us boys in front of the class and whacked us on the knuckles with a ruler if we misbehaved. I spent a lot of time in the first three grades enjoying fresh air and sunshine outside of the classroom, sitting on the porch. I learned to write with both hands on the blackboard after school from Mrs. Lau, my fifth grade teacher, and became proficient in cleaning blackboards. Mother always made me wear shoes to school and couldn't understand why they looked so new. I didn't tell her that I hid them in the bushes on the way to school, then put them back on while walking home. In the sixth grade, I transferred to Aliʻiolani Elementary School, an English Standard school. There I met the many friends and future Roosevelt classmates.

John Shaw and I walked to the beach from Kaimukī to borrow heavy surf boards from beach boys at the Moana Hotel. Since we couldn't lift, or even carry the heavy, solid, wood boards, they put them in the water for us; then we paddled out to the reef. With one foot on the board, and the other standing on the reef, John would push off and both of us would paddle like crazy to catch the wave. It was lots of fun, and the beach boys looked after us.

Then John and I decided to join the kids diving for coins at Aloha Tower when the luxury ocean liners, Lurline and Matsonia, docked. We caught pennies, nickels, and dimes, while the big kids got the quarters. We small kids took off all of our clothes and someone once stole our clothes from under the dock. We had no choice but to swim back to Waikīkī. We had never done anything like that before, but somehow made it. The beach boys thought it was funny, and found some old clothes for us to wear home.

Sometimes we'd get hungry and climb the coconut trees along the Ala Wai Canal. We'd husk them by beating them on the curb, drink the milk, break the shell and eat the contents. Other times we had to fight off the rats to get to a coconut, or climb another tree. What a life for a nine or ten year old!

With seven kids in the family, I had to go to work to help make ends meet. My first job at the age of eleven was a paper route in the Kaimukī and Kapahulu areas. I also worked as a part-time usher at Kapahulu Theater.

Before the war, I spent several summers visiting my Kauaʻi uncles, especially those who practiced dentistry, in Kōloa. I spent my days at the beach, digging ʻopihi with my pocket knife from the rocks and eating *limu* from the ocean. One day I saw what looked like human bones on the beach, and my uncle said that they were probably from ancient Hawaiian battles.

My uncle had a wonderful garden where he grew strawberries and Hawaiian sweet corn. His house was on a road in Poʻipu Beach with only three homes. I also spent two summers with my uncle, the physician, in Līhuʻe. He loved to hunt and kept two active hunting dogs. He had a huge vegetable garden and also grew roses, hydrangeas and gardenias. I learned about caring for roses and other things, like deciding to pursue a career in medicine if I didn't mind going on calls in the middle of the night. Thank goodness for my wonderful aunt, a registered nurse of Finnish descent from Michigan, who helped me through my early teen-age years.

I returned to Honolulu a few pounds heavier, and resumed my paper route. One day, someone started to pick on one of the younger paper carriers, and I told him to "Quit that!" He said, "Who's going to stop me?" I answered that I would, and as a result, left my blood on the sidewalk, stone wall, curb, street gutter, and all over the grass. So much for that! And the worst part, the bully lived on my paper route. Several days later, we ran into each other and, much to my surprise, he told me that he admired me for what I did, and if I had any problems with people like him to let him know, and he would take care of them. After completing the sixth grade at Aliʻiolani, I rode the HRT (Honolulu Rapid Transit) bus to Robert Louis Stevenson Intermediate School, also an English Standard school.

Sunday morning, Dec. 7, 1941, my mother was in the backyard of our Kaimukī home hanging laundry when she saw low-flying planes with a red ball under their wings. She called to us, and from the upstairs front porch, we watched a Navy destroyer off Waikīkī Beach dodging bombs. We saw heavy smoke and heard loud explosions from Pearl Harbor. When we turned on the radio, the announcer informed us that we were under attack by Japan. Father soon got a call from someone in his carpool who said they would come by and pick him up in about an hour and a half to report to their jobs at Pearl Harbor. Before Dad left, he gave me a .45 caliber Italian automatic pistol and said that if the Japanese landed troops, I should take my mother and the kids to Pālolo Valley, or up to Wilhelmina Rise. We didn't see my father for three days, and he was very quiet when he got home. It wasn't until years later that I learned that he had "never seen so much human flesh on the bulkheads in his life."

This was the first Christmas that we didn't have a Christmas tree...in fact, we hardly celebrated Christmas at all. Father worked as a Marine Engineer at Pearl Harbor. His job was to design and install marine boilers on all the ships and clear them to leave Pearl Harbor. During World War II, the Navy sent him to battle sites to oversee immediate repair of damaged ships to get them back into service. He also designed water distillation plants on recaptured islands, such as Wake, Tarawa, and Guam.

During WW II, I worked part-time as a night air-raid warden at Ali'iolani School and also kept my paper route. One of my Honolulu Star Bulletin customers, a retired Navy Lt. Commander, ran the Navy Commissary at Pearl Harbor. He offered me a summer job and when he told me what the pay was, I immediately said "Yes!" There, I learned to run the potato peeling machine, make huge quantities of salad and salad dressing, and made new friends with fellow workers who were Hawaiian, *Haole,* Portuguese, and Filipino.

The war made dramatic changes in our school lives at Stevenson. We had air raid, bomb shelter, and gas mask drills. I enjoyed going home with Alexis Lum during the drills, because his Portuguese mother was an excellent cook and we feasted on the goodies she baked. Besides Mrs. Gill, our French teacher, I was impressed by the shop teacher, the sweet-looking art teacher, and Mrs. Cook, who put up with our antics and taught us how to sing.

With the transition to Roosevelt during the war years, we met students from other schools, and held "court" on the patio. Occasionally, we tossed a few friends over the wall into the bushes. Mrs. Gill was then at Roosevelt, teaching Latin instead of French, so I enrolled in her class. I learned some interesting things from Miss Johnson, the Chemistry teacher. One of the last things I did was to make some hydrogen sulfide and casually leave it outside the lab door during school. What a terrible odor it made!

Fortunately, I had enough credits to graduate a year early, so I decided to skip my senior year. While at Roosevelt, I was recruited by Alexis Lum to join the Hawaii Defense Volunteers, a platoon of students from Roosevelt and Punahou schools. I served with Jim Templeton, Charles Amor, Ralph Cote, and Ben Kittle. What a great time we had going through the Blue Combat Jungle Training Course at Ka'a'awa! We learned to make a raft from our pants by tying the waist, inflating the legs and swimming with it and our gear, across Ka'a'awa Stream. We also learned to use explosives such as supercharges and concussion grenades. A Colonel, who was a famed jungle combat fighter, sometimes gave us thirty minutes of personal hand-to-hand combat training with a kill-or-be-killed-attitude. We also practiced landings using Am Track landing craft.

While most of my classmates were slaving in the pineapple fields, because of my allergies, I stayed behind to develop pictures for the Photo Club. I got my turn with pineapples later at the Del Monte Cannery, operating a machine that separated the large and smaller pineapples. After working at the cannery from 6 a.m. to 2:30 p.m. I worked at a gas station from 3:30 p.m. until it closed at 10:30 p.m. Then it was time to party until we got tired or ran out of money.

Since I had decided to graduate a year early, there was no money to buy a suit, much less cash for the senior prom or a date. Dad bought me a wool suit on sale and I wore the scratchy outfit for the first and last time at the ceremony. So much for my graduation in 1944! But I'll always feel a part of the class of '45.

After high school, I attended the University of Hawai'i before transferring to Missouri Valley College in Marshall, Missouri. By the time I graduated from dental school in 1954, I had married and had a daughter, Lianne. Another daughter and two sons followed; their ethnic backgrounds are English, Irish, Scottish, Welsh, Chinese and Hawaiian. We moved to Honolulu, where I practiced one year with my uncle, then spent two years as an Air Force dentist on Okinawa, Taiwan, the Philippines, and Iwo Shima. After leaving the service, I spent two years in a group practice in Kansas City, until I found a wonderful small town in northwest Missouri called Albany, (pop. 1200) where I practiced dentistry for 20 years. After selling my dental practice, the Missouri Department of Health offered me a position as Assistant Dental Director for the state of Missouri; in 1986, I became State Dental Director for Nebraska. By then I had divorced and remarried and we moved to Lincoln. After I retired, we returned to Missouri and started a free dental clinic for Medical Missions for Christ Community Health Center. I am a fellow in the International College of Dentists, a Fellow in the American College of Dentists, and have received numerous awards from the U.S. Public Health Association and the American Dental Association.

Lum with Father   *Lum with Mother*

ELLEN KAWAMOTO SHIKUMA

Like many Hawai'i residents, I am a third generation American of Japanese ancestry. My paternal grandmother, Kana Morishige, was a teenager when she arrived in Hawai'i from Yamaguchi, Japan. She accompanied her older sister, whose husband was contracted to work in the cane fields on Kauai. My paternal grandfather, Motojuro Kawamoto, was also in his teens when he arrived in Hawaii in 1887. The name Kawamoto literally means, in Japanese, "river source," so my parents decided to give my brother Frank and me complementary names. Frank was named after Sir Francis Drake; Ellen was from Sir Walter Scott's poem, Lady of the Lake. We were destined to cross water many times in our lives; of course, living in Hawai'i, we would have to cross an ocean to get anywhere.

I have four grandparents from four different places in Japan. Had they remained in Japan, they would never have met. Yet, in Hawaii, this was not uncommon, which is why many *Nisei* (second generation American-Japanese), often upon meeting, ask where in Japan their parents are from. It opens an interesting conversation and often leads to life-long friendships.

My maternal grandmother, Yoshino Sano, was a twenty-year old picture bride from Niigata, which is on the west coast of Japan. When she arrived in Hawai'i and met the man she had agreed to marry, he was not the man whose picture she held, but a much older man. She ran away, and with some friends from the ship, went to Kaua'i. It was there that she met my grandfather, Shigetaro Shibata, who was the same age as she when he accompanied his older sister and her husband to Kaua'i from Kumamoto in southern Japan. Shortly after they married, they moved to Kona, on the island of Hawai'i. With the help of a plantation manager who started his own coffee plantation, they opened a plantation store.

Grandfather Shibata learned English quickly and established a much needed general store in Hōlualoa, Kona, where he and my grandmother had six children, Mother being the oldest. A brother and sister died in infancy. When Mother was eighteen, the family moved to Honolulu where they operated a drug store, grocery store and butcher shop, one next to the other, on Artesian Street, all known as Shibata Store. Mother worked in the stores while attending Phillip's Commercial School. Grandfather hired my father as his accountant, which is how my parents met; not long after, they married.

Because there were no boys in the family, Grandfather later divorced Grandmother and returned to Japan, leaving her to raise the four children. He put someone he trusted in charge of the stores, but as it turned out, he sold the stores and ran off with the money, leaving Grandmother to fend for herself. She owned the home where the family lived, so was able to remain there for awhile until she was forced to sell it for much-needed cash. She then moved in with my parents.

Mother was a woman before her time; she was educated, and being bi-lingual, wrote business letters in both English and Japanese. She worked as a loan officer at a small Japanese bank in the River Street-Aala Park district. After I was born, mother took me to work everyday because I was being breast-fed. After a few months, her boss told her that she'd better stay home and take care of me because I was disrupting business. People who came to the bank often played with me and carried me around the office. That ended mother's banking career and she became a housewife. My brother, Frank came along nearly two years later.

When I was not yet five years old, I went to Castle Kindergarten, located down town, where Mother's good friend, Mrs. Takushi, worked. As I spoke both English and Japanese, and didn't know the difference, I often used both languages in a single sentence. I was my grandmother's translator when we went shopping, but never did learn her "pidgin-English," Hawaiian, Chinese, English, Portuguese, Russian and Japanese words all mixed up!

When the school year ended, my classmates went on to first grade, but since I was still only five years old, I couldn't go with them. As a result, I didn't want to go school. Mother finally took me to Aliʻiolani Elementary School, an English standard school, located just five blocks from our home in Kaimukī. The school year had already started when I met with the Principal, Mrs. Scobie. I sat in her office in a big chair while Mother waited outside. Mrs. Scobie talked to me and asked me questions, which I must have answered correctly, because the next thing I remember, I was sitting in a classroom full of children I didn't know.

I knew how to read, write, tell time, and also count up to one hundred; but it was hard for me was to make friends so I hung around my teacher, Mrs. Stearns. She encouraged me to play with the other children but I felt safer with her. By third grade, I had adjusted fairly well and had made friends with a lot of kids, many of whom would end up as classmates at Roosevelt. My brother, Frank, started at Aliʻiolani the same year. He had never gone to kindergarten and spoke mostly Japanese, so when we got home from school each day, I took over the role of his teacher.

Mother and Dad bought me a piano and hired their very good friend to be my teacher. I was eager to play songs that I sang, but nothing doing! I had to learn scales and play music with no words and also practice finger exercises...what a bore! Because I had to practice everyday for one whole hour under Mother's watchful eye, I began to hate piano lessons.

Everything was going fine in the fifth grade at Aliʻiolani until it was decided that I should start Japanese school. Enrolled in the Kaimukī 10th Avenue Japanese School, I would now have an extra hour of schooling. Japanese school was terrible! The kids talked pidgin and I didn't understand half of what was said, and nobody wore shoes except my brother and me. We were teased unmercifully, and if that wasn't enough, the kids ran up to us, made monkey faces, hit us, and even threw things at us. I was shocked and scared. I told mother, who went to school to let the Principal know what was happening to us. It only made things worse. Frank and I often found ourselves rolling on the ground fighting for our lives! Things got better when we decided to hide our shoes in the bushes on the way to Japanese School and pick them up on the way home. Finally, when we started to fight back, the kids left us alone.

My days were busy with Aliʻiolani School, Japanese School, including Saturday morning classes, one hour of piano practice, and lots of homework. There were many Japanese characters to learn and I think the only reason I studied was that I didn't want to be the class dummy. In Japanese school, girls and boys were separated in the classroom and seated according to how well they did. The first seat in the far side of the room next to the window was always occupied by the smartest boy; the smartest girl occupied the first seat near the door. My teacher was a student at the University of Hawai'i from Japan. He walked around with a stick and often tapped the boys on the head when they made mistakes; he pointed the stick at the girls. It was very embarrassing, but Mother said that's how it was in Japan. I protested and said I was an American and was not going to tolerate it!

In the seventh grade I left Ali'iolani and entered Robert Louis Stevenson School, an English standard intermediate school. Stevenson was different because each subject had a different teacher. Home Room was where we met each morning, and then moved on to another classroom. It was exciting and fun.

Because it was more convenient, I was enrolled at the Fort Street Japanese School, rather than returning to school in Kaimukī. It had a better reputation since it was run by the Hongwanji Mission.

Now my daily schedule was even busier and I had no time to play. Mother drove me to Stevenson every morning and picked me up at Japanese school every afternoon. There were piano lessons once a week, practice every day and lots of reading and homework to do at night. Mother called me the "no fun girl" because I complained so much about having "no fun!" Then she enrolled me in swimming and tap dancing classes at the YWCA on Saturday afternoons after Japanese School. Her idea of fun was to keep me so occupied I had no time to complain.

Dad was concerned that I wasn't having enough time of my own, so after much discussion and my pleading, he agreed to let me drop Japanese School at the end of the eighth grade. I was ecstatic! Now I was able to spend more time with my friends.

I regularly attended Sunday School at Makiki Castle Christian Church. It was called Makiki Castle because the architecture resembled a Japanese castle. The founder, Rev. Okumura, encouraged Japanese immigrants to become Christians in a familiar environment. Sunday sermons were given in English in the morning and Japanese in the afternoon. Sunday school, for young people from kindergarten through high school, was heavily attended. One reason was that Rev. Okumura operated a boarding school for boys and a separate one for girls. Their ages ranged from twelve through college, and many of the boys were from rural O'ahu and other islands and were required to attend Sunday school.

I wanted to become a Sunday school teacher, and enrolled in the Honolulu Bible Training School, located in a red brick building on King Street next to City Hall. Students attended an hour-long Bible class from eight to nine o'clock each Sunday morning and then we all quickly gathered in the auditorium for a morning service conducted by Rev. Waterhouse.

One Sunday morning in 1941, which happened to be December 7th, Rev. Waterhouse told us that there would be no worship service, as it was most important that we all go straight home, but he didn't tell us why. Standing at the curb with other students, expecting to be picked up by our parents, we saw planes streaking noisily overhead and remarked to each other that military maneuvers were getting so realistic! As the planes roared above, we heard a loud noise and saw a burst of fire near the Advertiser Building. Shortly afterward, fire engines roared past us to put out the blaze. Police cars zipped by and someone yelled out... "Hey kids! Go Home!" We just stood there in amazement, watching all the excitement, not knowing what to do until a friend rushed by in his Eagle Scout uniform and hollered, "You better catch a bus and get home fast because Japan is bombing us." Stunned, I ran across the street to catch a trolley when I realized that Frank was probably still at church, so I went looking for him. The church was open and there were a few people there, but Frank wasn't among them. I learned that our grandfather had picked him up and taken him to his home on Sheridan Street, so I walked over there. Everyone was overjoyed to see me as they were all very worried. Although they were not supposed to use the telephone, they called our parents to tell them that we were safe. Grandmother Kawamoto walked us to the bus stop taking a very circuitous route, walking through all the neighbors' backyards. The family thought it was safer for grandmother to take us rather than grandfather, or my uncles, as she would be looked on as a mama-san going home from work, rather than a man who might be considered a suspect. As soon as she got us safely on the bus, she disappeared and we made it home safely.

Classes did not start until February, 1942, when Kaimukī kids returned to Ali'iolani Elementary School for afternoon classes held from 12:30 p.m. to 4:00 p.m. I soon realized how the war was going to impact our lives because we had no extra-curricular activities, like dancing at lunchtime or any special classes. It would certainly be "no fun!"

Life at home had also changed. Dad didn't take us to the beach after work any more; he and my uncles were busy building a bomb shelter in the backyard. When it was completed, it was a cozy underground room with a front and back door. Dad planted sweet potato vines over it, and in a couple of weeks, it was completely camouflaged. We slept overnight just once when there was an air raid alarm in the middle of the night. It was a great place to hide, read and nap.

The September, 1942, news of the Pacific war was not good and there were all kinds of shortages... toilet paper, rice, milk, and other things we took for granted before the war. Now there were long lines at the stores whenever it was rumored that there was a shipment of something... anything! One time, on the way to a store on River Street, I found my grandmother standing in a line surrounded by soldiers and sailors. It turned out that there were two lines…one for rice leading into the store, and another line, for men going upstairs. Somehow she just got in the wrong line!

In spite of wartime conditions, Theodore Roosevelt High School started shortly after Labor Day. Those of us from Stevenson joined students that came from other intermediate schools in Honolulu: Kaimukī, Washington, Central, and Kalākaua. They had all passed the required "English Standard" test. My sophomore year was spent making new friends and getting used to different teachers for each new subject. These classes opened a whole new world, and I knew then that someday "when the war was over" I was going to see that world! Home Economics was a class I enjoyed because there was no homework and we could cook, sew and work together in little groups. To broaden our experience, our teacher arranged a visit to Kamehameha School for Girls. We arrived by bus and were welcomed by the girls with refreshments, followed by a tour of the school and residences. What a surprise! The girls lived in apartments with a house mother and were responsible for a "real baby!" That was their home economics real life class! We bathed a baby doll... they bathed, fed and cared for a real baby!

During our junior and senior years, all "able bodied" students joined other high schools to aid in the war effort by working in the pineapple fields every Monday. We rode in a large truck to and from the fields at Wahiawā. An incident that makes me laugh whenever I think about it was the occasion when Betty Chapson and I learned, that because we were younger than most of our classmates, we were being paid ten cents an hour less. We felt we were working as hard as the older kids, so we goofed off by crouching down between the plants and talking without being seen by the *luna*. After a while, we realized that it was suddenly very quiet. It was *pau hana* time and as we stood up, we saw the truck disappear over the ridge. There was nothing we could do except start hiking up the hill and hope that we would be missed. After what seemed an eternity, we saw the truck coming back. Betty and I decided that ten cents an hour wasn't worth being left behind.

After that experience, I decided to work at the cannery instead. I'm not sure which was worse as selecting pineapple slices for canning was not easy. Luckily I worked between experienced women, so I didn't slow down the production line too much. Canning required choosing slices for the proper cans as they moved down along the belt. After working at the cannery a couple of weeks, I developed a rash. That ended my cannery career and I spent the rest of my volunteer days folding bandages for the Red Cross.

During my junior and senior years I had a job as a cashier in the cafeteria. It was a great job! Because I received a free lunch, I could use my allowance to go shopping on my own. It gave me great pleasure to be able to buy a snakeskin handbag and matching high heeled shoes with my own money.

Of course I studied and did my homework, but never made the honor roll. I was too busy with extra curricular activities. For all three years, I was Class Representative on the Student Council; and ushered for the various evening programs at the Roosevelt auditorium. Since it was still wartime, there were many productions arranged by the Army entertainment unit, which was billeted in buildings in back of the school. I saw Maurice Evans, the famous Shakespearian actor, in his portrayal of Hamlet. The school was treated to after school dances by some of the Big Bands traveling through Honolulu. It was a thrill to dance to the music of Artie Shaw, Glenn Miller, Ray Anthony, Les Brown, Eddie Duchin and Tommy Dorsey; however, as I recall, very few of the boys were good dancers.

On April 12, 1945, President Franklin Delano Roosevelt died. It was traumatic for students and teachers alike. We were dismissed from class, and as we walked to the bus stop, we were all in tears. The war was still going on and now we had a new President, Harry Truman, of whom we knew very little. Finally, on May 8, 1945, the war in Europe was over. In June, we graduated with the war in the Pacific still raging. The future was uncertain, especially for the boys. Everyone I knew was planning to enter the military or college... if not the University of Hawai'i, somewhere on the Mainland. Graduation was a joyful, but somewhat sad occasion. It was the end of a special and happy part of our lives.

I graduated from the University of Hawaii in 1949 and married Henry Shikuma, a WW2, 442nd veteran, in August. We honeymooned in New York City while attending graduate school. We returned home briefly with our MA degrees, and in 1954 returned to live in New York City. I found employment with Pan American World Airways and worked my way from a ticket agent at the Fifth Avenue ticket office, to manager in Marketing Training, then to manager of Management Resources in Corporate Personnel. I was also able to fulfill my dream "to see the world!" Henry met and hit it off with Walt Kelly of "Pogo" fame and worked with Kelly on "Pogo" until Kelly's death in 1973. For the next two years, he carried on the strip with Kelly's son and widow. Henry passed away in 1985. I remained in New York and after retiring from the airline, returned to Honolulu in 1992. I now live in Kahala Nui, a retirement home where several of my high school classmates also reside.

The Kawamoto Family

Ellen and Frank

WILLIAM "TEX" HAYS

Since I have never done a genealogical search, I'm not sure of my ethnicity, but I think I'm probably a third English, a third Scotch, and a third Irish. My Mom's mom, Grandma McPherson, was originally from London. One of ten children, she became a governess and traveled all over Europe and Africa before coming to America to visit her sister, Aunt Jessie, and husband, Uncle Albert. There she met her first husband, Edward Palmer; they had a daughter, Mary Louise, my mother. Edward Palmer died in a fight on the San Francisco docks not long before the 1906 earthquake. I don't know what his ethnicity was, but Mom always thought she was part gypsy.

Later, Grandma met Mr. MacPherson, who was from Honolulu, and worked for the Star Bulletin. He convinced Grandma to move to Honolulu with her little daughter. In 1910 they got married, and a year later they had a little girl; they named her Jeannette, and in 1913, Alice was born.

As they were living in Kalihi at the time, the first school Mom attended was Kalihi Waena. She graduated from eighth grade along with Alvin Issacs, who later played in Harry Owens band. In 1939, Alvin and the band performed in Dallas and were partly responsible for our move to Honolulu.

When Mom was fifteen and a sophomore at McKinley High School, her step-father said she had to quit school and get a job to help support the family. She went to work in the lingerie department of Liberty House on Fort St. in downtown Honolulu.

Mom was still in her teens when she met and married a soldier stationed at Schofield Barracks, and when he was transferred to Texas, she followed. A baby girl they named Juanita was born to them there. When Juanita was only about two years old, her father abandoned his family and left them desolate in Dallas. That's where Dad met and fell in love with Mom and little Juanita; they married and he took them to his home in Longview.

It was in Longview, in an apartment above a garage, that I was born on April 30, 1927. Dad, William Edgar Hays, was born in Rusk County, Texas, and although he had only gone to the eighth grade, he was ambitious and work-oriented. In 1929, my brother, Robert Hays, came along, and in June of 1933, my youngest brother, Dickie, was born prematurely. Mom fell from the chair she was standing on while reaching for something and was rushed to the hospital; Dickie was born one and a half months early.

Mom's mother, Grandma MacPherson, and her two sisters, Jeannette and Alice, came from Honolulu to stay for awhile. Jeannette did not like Texas one bit and after a brief stay, she returned to Honolulu.

This was in 1929, during the height of the great 1929 depression. Dad was then working as a waiter in downtown Dallas. Mom worked part-time at the Sears catalogue plant filling catalogue orders as she zipped along the plant floor on a pair of roller skates. Still, both salaries couldn't provide enough food for the family of Grandma, Aunt Alice, Mom, Juanita, Bobby, Dad and me. To supplement our meager diet, Dad brought home left-overs from the café kitchen, like pieces of steak and bread slices which he rescued from the scrap barrel. It all helped.

Sometime in 1932, things got so desperate in our house food-wise, with Grandma and Aunt Alice still with us that our parents sent the three older kids, Juanita, Bobby, and me, to stay with relatives in East Texas.

One day I was in the outhouse... no one had plumbing in that area... and a horse came snuffling at the door. I shooed her away, and when my uncle saw the horse running he came out and grabbed me and said I had done wrong chasing the horse away because she was pregnant and could have miscarried. How was I to know, being city-bred and all? He said to get him a peach limb as he was going to whip me! When Mom and Dad heard about the incident, they took us away.

Grandma MacPherson and Aunt Alice moved back to Honolulu around 1937. Not long after returning to Hawai'i, Aunt Alice met and married Lake Bellinger, who worked at the Bishop Bank, while she worked at First Federal Savings and Loan on Fort Street.

In 1939, Harry Owens and his band came to Dallas for a gig at the Aldolfos Hotel. Mom knew a few of the band members, including Alvin Issacs, with whom she'd attended Kalihi Waena school, the two Tavares brothers, and a few of the hula dancers. She and Dad went to the show and afterward, at about 2:00 a.m., brought some of the band members to our house. I remember being awakened and hugged by these beautiful Hawaiian ladies. From then on, all we talked about was moving to Hawaii. Somehow, my Aunts, Grandma, and Uncle Lake scraped together $800 which they sent to Mom so she could move the whole family from Dallas to Honolulu.

We started that epic journey with a four-day bus ride to Los Angeles. Then we boarded the S.S. Lurline and sailed up to San Francisco before starting out across the Pacific to Hawai'i. The ship was divided into classes, first class being the finest. We were in cabin class and the classes were separated by heavy solid doors. Somehow, I managed to meet another twelve year old, Dick Clissold, who was traveling first class. It was the beginning of a lifelong friendship.

When we pulled into Honolulu Harbor in November, 1939, Aunt Jeannette came out on the pilot boat to greet us with an armful of lei. She and Grandma were living in a huge, old house on Kalākaua Avenue, just Waikīkī of the Ala Wai bridge, next door to the Black Cat Cafe and across Kalākaua from the outdoor skating rink.

I was immediately enrolled in Stevenson Junior High School. Juanita entered Roosevelt High School as a junior, the youngest in her class and graduated at age sixteen in 1941. Bobby went to Lincoln Elementary School in fifth grade and Dickie to Jefferson Elementary in Waikīkī, all English Standard Schools.

All six of us moved in with Aunt Jeannette and Grandma, until we could find a place of our own. Dad got a job with Spence Weaver selling hot dogs from a wagon called Swanky Franky's. About that time, we rented a house on Makiki Street, two doors down from the Hawai'i Sugar Planters' Association Experimental Station, and across the street from the Buddhist Temple. I walked to Stevenson every day with some of my new friends.

During social studies, we had dancing lessons, I guess to gentle our exuberant souls. I think they were held on the third floor, at the top of a very old building, and the floor actually shook when we danced.

After working a few months for Spence Weaver's Swanky Franky's, Dad got a job at Pearl Harbor as a plumber's assistant. This was early 1940, not long after we moved into the house on Makiki Street. During this time I worked as a stock boy at Fuller Brush Co. on Kapi'olani Blvd. two or three days a week after school. The manager, Mr. Hastings B. Pratt, was also my Boy Scout Master in Troop Four. We held meetings at a little park on O'ahu Ave. in Mānoa.

Life was good; I loved my new home and had lots of new friends. Because of my drawl, I acquired the nickname of "Tex," by which I'm still known. Everything went along so smoothly that it was hard to believe there was a war going on in Europe, or that we would instantly be drawn into it. But that was exactly what happened on Dec. 7, 1941 at 8:00 a.m. on Sunday morning. We heard a lot of noise and planes were flying overhead so we turned on the radio to find out what was happening. There we heard the voice of Web Edwards repeating over and over: "This is the real McCoy. Take cover. We're being attacked by Japan." Our neighbor, Mr. Camara, came out into the street and shook his fist at the planes flying overhead with the rising sun under their wings.

Around 8:30 a.m., several big black cars pulled into the driveway of the Buddhist Temple across the street. Men in black suits jumped out and rounded up all the priests and students who were there. I think they were taken to Sand Island in the middle of Honolulu Harbor, where a camp was set up to detain them. By nightfall, the U. S. Army had moved into the temple with guard shacks and barbed wire.

There was a call on the radio for all personnel to report to Pearl Harbor, both military and civilians. Dad left immediately, and when he finally came home about midnight, we heard him throwing up in the bathroom. He said later it was because of all the horrible death and destruction he had seen. He worked at Ford Island, right in the middle of Pearl Harbor.

The next day martial law was declared and the military took complete control of everything. Blackout was enforced from sundown to sunup, no one allowed on the streets without a pass, and any lights showing were shot out by neighborhood air raid wardens. All vehicle lights were blacked out, except for a small two-inch circle of blue. No busses ran and schools closed down for several months.

My friend, Dick Clissold, often invited me to his house in Mānoa to spend the night. Because there were no lights, everyone went to bed early. After the rest of his family was asleep, Dick and I sneaked out of his third floor room, climbed down the roof, and headed down Armstrong Way to meet "the gang" on O'ahu Ave. We all got together in front of Jock McIntyre's house: Jock, Pete Nottage, Dick and I, the St. John brothers, Shirley Tavares, Wanda Grant, the Christy brothers, George and Albert, and Jimmy Wooley. We were just kids hanging out, telling stories and evading the military police, and our parents.

The days were pretty much the same, just hanging out with friends, until one day Mrs. St. John said, "Enough of this no school business," and she started a class on her *lānai*. I can't remember what she taught us, but we had to give up sitting on the curb doing nothing.

Somehow I got a job with Burns Messenger service on Beretania St. in downtown Honolulu. I helped the truck driver deliver Liberty House purchases. Rikino Fukamoto was the driver and he had an old '28 Chrysler roadster parked in his driveway that needed work, and since he didn't want to do it, he offered it to me. At fourteen years old I couldn't drive, but I accepted the car and somehow got it towed from his house in Nuʻuanu to my house on Makiki St.

I did some repair work to the rumble seat, which had been damaged by termites, got the motor running, and started backing up and going forward on our long driveway, teaching myself to drive. But I still needed better tires since the original ones were worn out. Dick Clissold said he knew where there were four tires the right size on an abandoned car above the track field at Punahou School. We went up and took the tires off the car and rolled them down the road to my house. Punahou School had been taken over by the U. S. Army Corps of Engineers for the duration, and we had to pass the guard at the gate. He asked if we had permission to take the tires and we said we did. Then he said he had to take our names and addresses, which we gave him.

After we got to my house, we felt remorse for having lied, especially since we had given our real names and addresses. We went back and confessed, and the guard told us to report to his superior. So down into the basement we went. The guy in charge of the guards, I think he was one of the Kahanamoku brothers, said we would have to turn the tires in to the depot down at Ala Moana, where the shopping center is today. So we dutifully took the old tires down and threw them on a huge pile of rubber being collected for the war effort. Then we put the new tires on my car.

After driving up and down the driveway enough times I felt confident that I could pass the driving test. I had just turned fifteen, so I asked my sister, Juanita, to check me out. I drove up around Roosevelt and back and she said I could do it. So down to the Bethel Street Police station I went. Joe Ikiole, the very fat cop, was my instructor. When he got into the passenger side, the little car tilted way over. I managed to do well on the driving tests, but when we went inside and I was told, "Read the chart on the wall," I couldn't. Joe told me to go home, have my parents take me to get glasses, and then come back. I got the glasses, went back, read the chart, and got my license.

The summer of 1942 I got a real, forty-hour-a-week job at Dole Pineapple Cannery on Dillingham Blvd. During the weekends, my friends and I would pile into the roadster and head for the beach. The entire island was ringed with barbed wire but there were small spaces where you could go through to get in the water. Everyone chipped in with gas coupons or money for gas.

When we finally did go back to school to the ninth grade at Stevenson, bomb shelters had been dug into the grounds and we all had to have our gas masks strapped over our shoulders at all times. We had our graduation ceremonies in June of '42, and I was one of three students chosen to give a speech, along with Jane Steen and Jim Templeton. I can't remember what I spoke about.

In September, we started the tenth grade at Roosevelt; Dudley Pitchford and I were the only two sophomores with cars. He had a little MG, smaller even than my roadster. The campus was surrounded by barbed wire as the Navy had taken over the gym and the athletic field.

At Roosevelt, I made friends with Mack Hill, Dick Beers, Emmett Hazlett and Warry Gunderson, (we called ourselves the "Big 5") and partied every weekend. We had a blast! Of course, blackout was in force from sundown to sunup, so we couldn't be on the street. We just stayed at the party, wherever it was.

Every Monday we had to work in the pineapple fields as the regular workers had been drafted into the military. We were taken to Wahiawā in a old truck with benches lined up in the back. We worked hard but what I remember most were the guava fights we had during lunch break.

I drove my little '28 roadster from the summer of '42 to December '43, when I raffled it off at a Gripers' Club meeting and made $112.50. Even my Grandmother bought a chance. Then I bought Clem McSwanson's '32 Ford V8 convertible very cheap, because the second gear needed replacing. After repairing it, I drove it until 1947, when I left for the mainland and college; then I sold it for $300.

During my years at Roosevelt, we partied a lot. The war was still going on, Hawai'i was still under Martial Law, and the Army had control of everything! Still, there were the usual high school activities such as football games, rallies, basketball games, dances on the patio, plays in the auditorium; after school there were beaches to explore, waves to body surf, or card games to play on the lawn at the Outrigger Canoe Club at Waikīkī. Each year my grades dropped a little, and I even flunked Spanish. To me, school was the place to meet my friends and plan our next outing.

On graduation night in June, 1945, we all went to our school dance at Hawaiian Town on Kapi'olani Boulevard. My date was Cissy Jensen; Emmett's date was Pat Kirshbaum. We had Military passes which allowed us to be out after curfew.

With school over, it was time to think of college, at least until I went into the service. It was great not to worry about home work and studying and grades anymore, but still, those years at Roosevelt were special and I will always cherish them.

Soon after graduation I was drafted into the Army and spent thirteen months with Uncle Sam, stationed on O'ahu. After my discharge, I attended Farragut College, a small institution in northern Idaho, along with classmates Mack Hill and Warren Gunderson. There I met my future wife, Betty, at a dance. Later I transferred to the University of Oregon at Eugene, but kept up my romance with Betty and after I graduated in 1951, we were married. Having worked summers for Sears Roebuck in Spokane, I applied for a job and was hired in their Management Training Program. In 1959, just before statehood, I transferred to Sears in Hawai'i. Three of our four children were born in Spokane, the youngest was born in Kailua. After thirty-five years in various positions, I retired from Sears in 1986. Betty passed away in January of 2011.

Tex and brother Bobby

*Classmates Mack Hill, Emmett Hazlet,
Tex Hays, Dick Beers, Warren Gunderson*

Epilogue

It was June 13, 1945, and the George R. Carter Auditorium was filled to capacity with parents, relatives, friends, teachers, and students. When the graduation ceremony ended, the classmates rose from their seats for the last time to sing the alma mater; there wasn't a dry eye among them. Clutching their diplomas, they raised their voices loud and clear as the words "…and pledge to keep our colors high through all the years to be…." echoed through the hall. With the ending words "…All hail! Hail! Hail! students from the class of '45 raised their arms high in the air and cheered.

In the Roosevelt class of 1945, there were approximately 340 students who actually graduated. The number was reduced as many students dropped out in their senior year because they joined the Merchant Marine or a branch of the military service; some were sent to the mainland for the duration of the war; others left to take lucrative defense jobs.

In the ensuing months, many of the young men were drafted, as the war, although winding down, was still going on in the Pacific. On August 6 of that year, the atomic bomb was dropped on Hiroshima and Nagasaki. On August 15, Japan formally surrendered. After their stint in the service, most of the male graduates took advantage of the G. I. Bill of Rights and pursued the higher education it offered.

For the many graduates who left to attend colleges on the mainland, it was an ordeal to be allowed to travel. After an interview with a Navy Commander, if permission was granted, a priority was assigned to the person who was required to be packed and ready to depart at a moment's notice. As no advance notice of sailing time was given, someone was required to be available to answer the phone at all times, in many cases for as long as two months.

A surprisingly large number of graduates from the Class of '45 attended college. Most who did, went to the University of Hawai'i. Others enrolled in top-notch institutions such as Harvard, George Washington University in Washington D. C., Northwestern, Wellesley, Stanford, and Columbia. Others attended colleges and universities in Colorado, Oregon, New Mexico, Ohio, Oklahoma, California, Michigan, Wisconsin, and Iowa. Football players were attracted to St. Mary's College in Moraga, California. A few attended small, little-known schools such as Farragut College in Idaho, and Bethany College in West Virginia. Armstrong Business College in Berkeley, California, was popular with *wāhine* planning to pursue secretarial careers. Many of the male graduates became doctors, dentists, or lawyers.

Despite, or perhaps because of the war, with its many restrictions, and partial take-over of the campus, the Roosevelt class of 1945 experienced a special bonding that has continued for over seventy years. Although many of the students are no longer living, and many have resided on the mainland since their high school days, as a whole they have kept in touch and attended class reunions over the years.

Early reunions were held at Japanese tea houses, where guests sat on *tatami* mats on the floor, served by Japanese ladies clad in elegant silk kimonos. The fare usually consisted of tempura, sashimi, smoked salmon and other Japanese delicacies with hot sake as the beverage. The twenty-fifth reunion was a dinner-dance at the Kāne'ohe Yacht Club on the Windward side of O'ahu. As so many people came from the mainland to participate in the nostalgic get-togethers, the reunions grew from a one-night affair to nearly a week of activities. The 55th reunion in 2000 included a day of golf at Bay View Golf Park in Kāne'ohe, a catered cocktail party at a private home, a morning cruise off Waikīkī and Pearl Harbor on the Star of Honolulu which included a continental breakfast, buffet luncheon, and entertainment. On the following day, a tour of 'Iolani Palace was conducted by classmates who were Palace docents, followed by a lunch at Café Laniākea at the Y.W.C.A. across the street. The final day featured a *lu'au* in the spacious yard of a class member. Held every five years, other reunions featured banquets at the Cannon Club at Fort Ruger, the Hale Koa Hotel at Fort De Russey, and nine-course dinners at Hee Hing, a popular Chinese restaurant.

Many alumni attend an annual reunion held each February in Las Vegas which combines five consecutive classes. Based at the California Hotel, each class is provided with a hospitality suite where classmates gather for *kanikapila* and nostalgic reminiscing during the evening. For many years, the Class of '45 attracted the largest group from all the classes because of its talented musicians, singers, and dancers. The final night featured a banquet with top-notch entertainment for the combined classes.

Every event, no matter where it is held, ends with singing the alma mater, hands raised high, in honor of a place held dear to the hearts of those members of the Roosevelt High School class of '45. All Hail! Hail! Hail!

GLOSSARY OF HAWAIIAN WORDS

Hawaiian definitions from the Dictionary by Mary Pukui and Samuel Elbert.

akule. Big-eyed or goggle-eyed scad fish.

hānai. Foster or adopted child; to adopt

haole. White person, Caucasian. Formerly any foreigner ; foreign, introduced.

haole koa. (*Cordia sebestena*). An evergreen West Indian shrub or small tree.

hapa haole Part white person.

hau. Lowland tree that grows near the water. (Hibiscus tiliaceus)

hemo. Loose, separated, open. To loosen, undo, unfasten. Taken off, as clothes.

hiki. Can, be able to.

hikieʻe. Large, Hawaiian couch.

huki. To pull, as on a rope; to draw, stretch, reach.

hukilau. Seine; to fish with a seine. Pull ropes.

huki pau. Finish pulling.

kamani. (*Calophyllum inophyllum*) *T*ree found on shores of Indian and Pacific ocean.

kamau. Card game, similar to whist. Trump; to trump.

kanikapila. Play music.

keiki. Child; offspring, descendent, boy, son.

ki. Ti. A woody plant. (*Cordylinetermanalis*) Found from tropical Asia to Hawaiʻi.

kiawe. Algaroba tree. (*Proposis*) From tropical America; in Hawaiʻi since 1828.

kolohe. Mischievous, naughty. Rascal.

konohiki. Head of *ahupuʻaha* under chief. Land or fishing rights under his control.

kuaʻaina. Country person. Rustic, of the country.

kumu. Teacher, model, primer, pattern.

lānai. Porch,veranda.

laulau. Packages of ti or banana leaves containing pork, beef, fish, taro tops etc.

lei ana ika. Adorned with.

limu. A general name for all kinds of seaweed.

lua. Hole, grave, crater; toilet or outhouse.

luʻau. Young taro tops. A Hawaiian feast.

luna. High, upper, above. Foreman, boss, overseer.

makai. Ocean; toward the ocean.

mauka. Inland. Toward the mountains.

ʻoʻopu. General name for fishes included in the families *Eleotridae* and *Goblidae*.

ʻopihi. Limpet. Any of several species of *Helcioniscus*. Salted, dried abalone.

papio. A fish.

pau. Finished, ended, completed.

pau hana. Finish work.

pepeiao. Ear.

pikake. Arabian jasmine, introduced from India.

pipi kaula. Beef salted and dried in the sun.

poi. Hawaiian staff of life. Made from cooked taro, pounded and thinned with water.

pūneʻe. Moveable couch.

wahine. Woman, female.

wāhine. Women. Plural of woman.

weke. Goat fish.

Asian and Pigeon English words.

fu qua kon. Bitter melon. Used by Chinese for medicinal purposes.

furo. Japanese bath about 25 inches deep with square sides.

jook. Chinese rice soup often made with the carcass of a turkey or chicken. **mamasan.** Common term used to describe maids and housecleaners **manapua.** Shortening of the Hawaiian *mea ʻono puaʻa*, meaning, "delicious thing with with pork inside." The Chinese brought this dim sum item with them when they were brought over as plantation workers. This food usually consists of a white bun with a dark pink-colored diced pork filling.

palaka. A distinctive navy and white plaid fabric of heavy cotton worn by plantation workers.

pan tat. Cat fish

sampan. A flat-bottomed boat propelled by poles, oars (particularly a single, long oar called a *yuloh;* Sampan buses featured open-air sides with a platform roof and roll-down side curtains to fend off the wet side of the island's frequent rains.

see moi. Dried and seasoned fruit including plums, lemon peel, mango.

see qua. Type of squash, similar in shape to a cucumber, with deep ridges.

saimin. Japanese noodle soup.

tai chi. Chinese martial art.

tatami. Woven straw mat

Tis with hearts full of pride,

dear alma mater

We rise and sing to thee,

And pledge to keep our colors high

through all the years to be.

To thy name we promise to be loyal,

Ever faithful ever true,

Roosevelt to thee our song shall be,

All hail, hail, hail!

Printed in the United States
By Bookmasters